D1439154

LITTLE BOOK OF THE

RUGBY WORLD CUP

THE GREATEST SHOW ON EARTH

LITTLE BOOK OF THE
RUGBY WORLD CUP

First published in the UK in 2007. Updated in 2015

© G2 Rights Ltd 2015

www.G2ent.co.uk

Publishers Edward Adams & Jules Gammond

Printed and bound in Poland

ISBN 978-1-782815-45-7

Contents

Foreword

by BBC rugby correspondent Ian Robertson

I have covered all seven World Cups from the first in New Zealand and Australia in 1987 to the most recent in New Zealand in 2011.

They have grown in stature and global significance on every occasion and there is no doubt that the 2015 World Cup will be the biggest and best and attract the largest worldwide audience.

It is guaranteed to be a massive financial success but it is also going to be a tournament to savour from the opening match at Twickenham between England and Fiji to the Final six weeks later.

The Rugby World Cup is one of the biggest events in the sporting calendar alongside the Olympics and the FIFA World Cup. Of the seven previous win-

ners only one Northern hemisphere team has won - England in Sydney in 2003 when they beat Australia.

That day I came quite close to pro-

RIGHT Ian Robertson has seen it all in rugby and heads into his eighth World Cup

OPPOSITE With only seconds left on the clock, deep into extra time, Jonny Wilkinson dispatched a perfect drop goal to seal a 17-20 victory over Australia in the 2003 World Cup final ducing a half decent commentary when I described Jonny Wilkinson's drop goal to win the World Cup for England in the final minute of extra time.

It was at the same time, potentially, a commentary fraught with a very different outcome. Jonny had kicked 21 drop goals for England but all with his left foot. This was with his right foot.

I was perched in an eyrie in the back of the main stand about 60 metres from the near touch line. The drop goal was struck a further 40 metres from that near touch line in mid-field. As he kicked the ball, I grabbed my binoculars for reassurance and it was with great relief that I saw it was indeed Jonny and not Mike Catt that had hit the goal. He was some 100 metres away - a small dot on the horizon!

The final whistle blew and I knew I had not covered the most iconic moment in England's rugby history too badly when John Inverdale - a man not known for idle flattery - said, " I can safely say that wasn't the worst commentary you've ever done…"

Like the whole rugby world I am looking forward enormously to the 2015 World Cup. It promises to be a very special tournament.

Chapter 1

The World Cup

Humble beginnings

ALTHOUGH THE FIRST RUGBY World Cup was held in 1987, ever since the first Test matches, in 1871, sides across the world have claimed the unofficial title of the best rugby team on the planet.

At the start only England and Scotland battled for the title but by the 1920s it was accepted that the epic series between New Zealand and South Africa was deciding who were the unofficial world champions.

Other sides – most notably Wales in the early 1970s – laid claim to their unofficial title but for the decades either side of the war it was either the Springboks or the All Blacks who were the team to beat.

BELOW An early match between England and Scotland in the Athletic Grounds at Richmond, 1891

The closest rugby got to anointing an official world champion before 1987 was at the Olympic Games, where rugby was included in four Games between 1900 and 1928.

France won the first gold medal and USA the last before the Olympic committee removed rugby from their list of sports.

With football starting its World Cup in Uruguay in 1930, it was inevitable that rugby would go the same way at some point. Perhaps the only mystery is why it took so long?

The length of the time could probably be attributed to rugby's roots as an amateur sport.

Some leading nations were fervent campaigners of the amateur traditions right up until the game turned professional, in 1995. Some, like England, even opposed the World Cup when it was first mooted in the late 1970s, for fear of it leading to a professional game.

It was not until late 1983 that the Australian Rugby Union and New Zealand Rugby Football Union submitted written proposals to the International Rugby Board (IRB) for a World Cup.

Neither was aware of the other's proposal with Australia wanting to stage a tournament to coincide with their Bicentenary in 1988 and New Zealand proposing the previous year.

Both proposals were turned down but the two countries pooled their resources to conduct a feasibility study to be presented at the IRB's annual meeting in March 1985.

But it took the IRB until 1985 before they took their momentous decision, at their annual meeting in Paris, two years after the similar proposal was rejected.

New Zealand had been at the centre of the campaign for a World Cup since 1983, Australia joining the campaign a year later.

At the 1985 meeting - chaired by Australia's Dr Roger Vanderfield - it certainly wasn't a unanimous decision with the British and Irish unions initially sceptical, although today the Rugby

ABOVE During the 1924 Olympics, rugby was played at the Colombes Stadium in Paris

World Cup is one of the top three sporting events (behind the Olympics and the Football World Cup) in the world.

Only a two-thirds majority was in fact required at the IRB Executive and it was resolved to stage a 16-team tournament.

France were in favour of the proposal on one condition: that the Tournament would not be restricted to the eight IRB members but would involve other countries to enable the game to reach a broader audience.

No one at that 1985 meeting could have considered how quickly the Rugby World Cup would grow, and the multi-million pound event staged by Australia in 2003 – that captivated the tradition in the 1980s – the IRB announced the new tournament, after the New Zealand and Australia rugby unions presented their feasibility study. The IRB said: "This study was presented to the board and has been considered in detail by each member union. Following very full discussion, the board has agreed to proceed with the staging of a competition in 1987." Hardly the fanfare that you would expect today, but it still signalled the beginning of a tournament that has grown hugely each time. Those board members couldn't have imagined how it would have developed over the following 20 years.

They settled on 1987 as the year, for the first one, thereby avoiding any clash with the Olympic Games, FIFA World Cup or European Football Championship. This decision has been one of the key reasons for its success.

The first tournament was staged in May and June 1987, but by the time the 2011 tournament was set – for New Zealand – the IRB resolved to make the desired window September and October.

This decision over the months in which it is staged has met with dismay

countries across the world – was a stunning success.

So nervous was the IRB about the World Cup, initially there were no plans for a second World Cup, but today we couldn't imagine the rugby world without it.

In a rather understated way – as was

in the British and Irish unions as it means they cannot stage their lucrative November internationals every four years, having a big effect on their financial planning.

Back in 1987, the board set up a committee to control all aspects of the World Cup and appointed Australia and New Zealand to carry out the organisation and planning.

The five-man committee, chaired by England's former British and Irish Lion, John Kendall-Carpenter, also included Australia's Ross Turnbull, Keith Rowlands of Wales and Irishman Ronnie Dawson.

One person who played a key role in this journey was the late Vernon Pugh QC, the IRB and Rugby World Cup Ltd chairman. Pugh's energy and vision was instrumental in expanding the governing body to include 94 full members and in building the profile of the sport's showpiece event.

The 16 teams to participate in 1987 were invited by the IRB, in great contrast to the almost three-year qualification tournament that took place to decide the 20 teams that took part in 2003.

"I vividly remember watching the inau-gural World Cup as a gangly 16-year-old experiencing the first stirrings of its potential; secretly desiring but never truly believing that one day I may have the chance to participate," explained John Eales, who won the World Cup twice, in 1991 and 1999, in Gerald Davies' History of the World Cup.

"For me the World Cup cannot be defined by a single movement but by

LEFT John Eales holds the Webb Ellis trophy after the 1999 final between France and Australia which Australia won 35-12

the camaraderie, the passion and the excitement that the tournament encapsulates. There was something personally special about each of the tournaments in which I was involved."

Back in 1987 South Africa missed out, due to the political situation in the country. At the time New Zealand and Australia – where the first World Cup would be held – had a ban on the granting of visas to South African sports people. This didn't stop South Africa voting in favour of the tournament but the ban – due to the presence of apartheid in South Africa – meant they also missed the 1991 World Cup, making their debut – with victory – in 1995.

Ireland turned out to be one of the main opponents to the World Cup, fearing that it would signal the end to tours by the British and Irish Lions. They were one of the last nations to finally accept their invitation to take part.

BELOW The crowd cheers the South African Springbok team during a victory parade through Johannesburg, 1995

And to address some of those concerns the IRB went to great lengths to stress the amateur ethos of the first World Cup.

"The thing that interests us is the need to shore up rather than undermine the amateur ethos of the game. We probed this side very carefully and we have established a number of procedures so that the tournament remains very much on an amateur basis," said John Kendall-Carpenter, chairman of the IRB governing committee.

The Lions, of course, prospered in the professional, World Cup era, deciding to stage their tours two years before the World Cup, in each four-year cycle. So the Lions toured in 1997, 2001 and 2005, to fit in around the World Cup.

The IRB oversaw the establishment of a company, Rugby World Cup Ltd, to run the tournament, a system that still exists today.

"Of all the many matters discussed by the Board," Kendall-Carpenter, the Somerset headmaster added, "the new competition has to be a major part of rugby's future. The Board must control the tournament in all aspects. It is essential that we get everything right." How prophetic those words were.

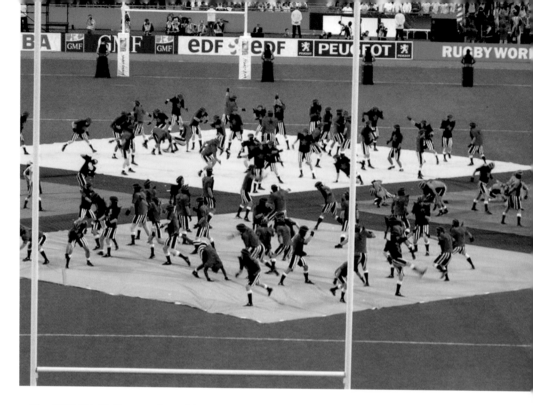

The 2007 World Cup was hosted by France, with matches also being held in Wales and Scotland. South Africa claimed their second title by defeating defending champions England 15–6.

The 2011 tournament was awarded to New Zealand in November 2005, ahead of bids from Japan and South Africa. The All Blacks reclaimed their place atop the rugby world with a narrow 8–7 win over France in the 2011 final.

Rugby World Cup Limited recommended to the IRB that the 2015 and 2019 World Cups be held in England and Japan, respectively, and in July 2009 it was announced that this proposal was adopted.

1987
The big kick off

IT WASN'T EXACTLY JUMPERS FOR goalposts, more like Rugby in the Raw when the World Cup finally kicked off in 1987... light years away from the 2007 event.

The game may have been amateur but the rugby was far from it, bringing some unforgettable matches and performances from some of the world's greatest players.

It was also a great success off the field with 600,000 fans coming through the turnstiles, at an average of 18,750 per match.

This prompted the chairman of the organising committee John Kendall-Carpenter to announce: "As far as I am concerned, the future is assured. We will have an unstoppable base for a tournament in 1991." At the time no-one had committed to a second World Cup.

"Rugby is not a world game at the moment," he added. "It's strong in certain parts of the world and other countries are being brought up to that standard."

Australia – the joint host with New Zealand – had just completed a Grand Slam in Europe and went into the tournament as one of the favourites.

RIGHT Wales went on to finish third in 1987 after beating England

But the 1987 World Cup was all about their joint hosts, New Zealand, as the All Blacks left an indelible mark on the Rugby World Cup.

The 16 World Cup finalists were made up of the seven IRB full board members – England, Scotland, Ireland, Wales, France, Australia, New Zealand – and nine invited sides. The only side excluded was South Africa, still exiled from many sports due to their apartheid political system.

With the World Cup only devised two years before, there simply wasn't time for the worldwide qualification tournament we see today.

Invitations were sent to: Argentina, Fiji, Italy, Canada, Romania, Tonga, Japan, Zimbabwe and the United States as the Board tried to bring member unions from all parts of the world.

But as the matches proved, those nine invited sides were unable to keep pace with the stronger top seven, producing a pretty lopsided pool stage, Japan, Tonga and Zimbabwe failing to win a match between them, and the real rugby only starting in the quarter-finals.

The seven top nations were joined by Fiji in those quarter-finals, the Fijians going down 31-16, at Eden Park, to France, who made it into the semi-finals along with Wales, Australia and New Zealand.

With New Zealand scoring 190 points in their three pool games and thrashing Scotland 30-3 in the quarters, Wales were their unfortunate opponents in the semis. The All Blacks cruised into the final with a 49-6 victory, Wales' Huw Richards becoming the first man to be sent off in a World Cup match.

New Zealand just failed to average 50 points a match at the first World Cup, summing up how they dominated.

England's tournament ended in the last eight when they lost 16-3 to Wales

BELOW France on their way to beating Australia in the semi-final of the 1987 tournament

and were described as "dreadful" by the Daily Telegraph's rugby correspondent, John Mason.

"They were shorn of ideas, tactical appreciation and all three Wales tries came from English mistakes."

In the semi-final – between France and Australia – the crowd were privileged to see one of rugby's great tries in the history of the game, Serge Blanco finishing off a length of the field move to take his side through 30-24.

Australia held the lead three times in a pulsating match, before Blanco struck for the final time.

The French – who came into the game after winning a Five Nations Grand Slam – were sublime and in the Sunday Telegraph John Reason said; "I never thought I would live to see a game to rival the one between the Barbarians and New Zealand in 1973, but this one did. So much was happening in so many places, for so much of the time that this game will be remembered as long as the World Cup is played."

The only result verging on a shock came in the third-place play-off with Wales triumphing 22-21 over Australia.

In the final, France failed to find their semi-final form, New Zealand storming to the title with a 29-9 victory.

The first final – in front of a capacity 46,000 crowd at Eden Park – wasn't a classic but they rarely are with All

BELOW New Zealand get ready for their semi-final against Wales by performing their haka

Blacks kicker Grant Fox – who scored 126 points at the tournament – running the game, and slotting six successful kicks at goal. Captain David Kirk also scored a try, along with Michael Jones and John Kirwan. The All Blacks dominated from start to finish to become the first side to lift the Webb Ellis Cup.

There was scant consolation for France in the latter of the final stages when Pierre Berbizier ran in the only French try.

New Zealand were also lucky to have the man of the tournament, openside flanker Michael Jones, marauding through the tournament, with a series of memorable displays.

New Zealand's domination of the first World Cup came after they lost captain Andy Dalton in the run-up to the tournament, a certain Sean Fitzpatrick taking his place in the team and Kirk, as skipper.

"We had lost a Test to France the year before and they had won the last two Five Nations. What evolved in the game was not our prettiest rugby but it was our best. France asked a lot of us," said Kirk.

"Having seen France play Australia in that epic semi-final, we felt they had

left something on the field.

"The game sped by and the French were pretty physical. But once I scored I had a gut feeling and knew we'd be champions.

"When the whistle went, there was no massive relief moment as we knew we were going to win. I just remember making a dash off the field – in the days when spectators could still run on.

"Lifting the trophy was neither a real buzz nor an anti-climax. There was a touch of melancholy. It must be how people feel at the top of Everest. They only have 20 minutes there and won't ever be back. The only way back is down.

"But that melancholy was overwhelmed by joy. It was all pretty amazing."

1987 WORLD CUP STAT ATTACK

GROUP A

Australia	19	England	6
USA	21	Japan	18
England	60	Japan	7
Australia	47	USA	12
England	34	USA	6
Australia	42	Japan	23

Australia and England qualify

GROUP B

Canada	37	Tonga	4
Wales	13	Ireland	6
Wales	29	Tonga	16
Ireland	46	Canada	19
Wales	40	Canada	9
Ireland	32	Tonga	9

Wales and Ireland qualify

GROUP C

New Zealand	70	Italy	6
Fiji	28	Argentina	9
New Zealand	74	Fiji	13
Argentina	25	Italy	16
Italy	18	Fiji	15
New Zealand	46	Argentina	15

New Zealand and Fiji qualify

GROUP D

France	20	Scotland	20
Romania	21	Zimbabwe	20
France	55	Romania	12
Scotland	60	Zimbabwe	21
Scotland	55	Romania	28
France	70	Zimbabwe	12

France and Scotland qualify

QUARTER-FINALS

New Zealand	30	Scotland	3
Wales	16	England	3
France	31	Fiji	16
Australia	33	Ireland	15

SEMI-FINALS

New Zealand	49	Wales	6
France	30	Australia	24

THIRD PLACE PLAY-OFF

Wales	22	Australia	21

WORLD CUP **FINAL**

New Zealand	29	France	9

LEADING TRY SCORERS

C Green (NZ)	6
J Kirwan (NZ)	6
M Harrison (Eng)	5
J Gallagher (NZ)	5
A Whetton (NZ)	5
D Kirk (NZ)	5

LEADING POINTS SCORERS

G Fox (NZ)	126
M Lynagh (Aus)	69
G Hastings (Scot)	50
J Webb (Eng)	43
D Camberabero (Fr)	37
S Koroduadua (Fiji)	35

1991
Second time around

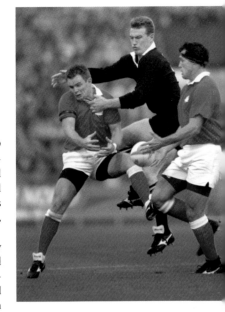

AFTER THE FIRST RUGBY WORLD Cup was held – in 1987 – in the southern hemisphere, it was clear the second event would move to the north and where better than in the Five Nations countries of England, Wales, Scotland, Ireland and France.

So much had changed in the rugby world since 1987, as the game raced towards professionalism, and significantly on the pitch England had emerged – once more – as a real force in the game.

England merely made up the numbers in 1987 but with a new coach – Geoff Cooke – and a new captain in Will Carling they had won a Five Nations Grand Slam in 1991, arriving at the tournament as one of the favourites.

They had the added incentive of the fact that the final this time would be played at their home ground of Twickenham.

Commercialism also arrived at the World Cup in a far bigger form than four years earlier. Television coverage had amounted to 28 hours in 1987 but four years later it was more than 100 hours, sponsors and suppliers providing support to the tune of £10 million, allowing the gross income to rise to just short of £40 million.

RIGHT New Zealand, here against Canada, with John Kirwan battling for the ball, failed to retain their title, losing in the semi-final

That income was turned into a profit of almost £25 million, up considerably from the £120,000 made in 1987.

Many things might have changed but one thing that hadn't was the form of New Zealand's Michael Jones, who after scoring a try in the first game of the 1987 competition – against Italy – repeated the trick in 1991 as the World Cup opened with England v New Zealand at Twickenham.

The 18-12 win by New Zealand meant that England would have to take a hard road to the final. As others enjoyed the green pastures of Twickenham, England were forced to overcome France in Paris and Scotland in Edinburgh to take their place alongside Australia for the second World Cup final.

Many people chose to blame England's decision to move from a forward-dominated game plan to one which tried to master the arts of expansive rugby. But the fact that they fell at the final hurdle was due more to the Herculean efforts they had to summon in the matches before, just to make the final.

In the end their change of tactics didn't bring a solitary try, prop Tony Daly

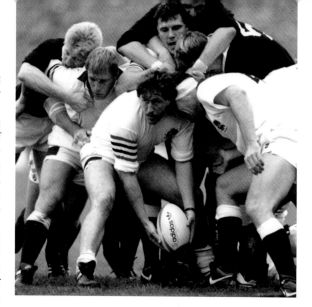

scrambling the only one of the game in the first half, following a lineout.

David Campese didn't score but it was always hard to keep the great Aussie wing out of the game. When he batted down a pass meant for the overlapping Rory Underwood, Twickenham held its breath, only to see referee Derek Bevan give a penalty, rather than the penalty try all of England craved.

"I'm happy England chanced their arm that day but I can't believe that people still go on about that one, insisting that Campo cost Underwood the score," said Australia captain Nick

ABOVE Mike Teague sets up the ball in the game against Scotland during the 1991 semi-final

Farr-Jones.

"I don't know why as there's no way Underwood would have scored. He still had miles to cover and the defence would have come across."

England's only points came from the boot of Jonathan Webb, and Australia were home, Farr-Jones receiving the Webb Ellis Cup from Her Majesty the Queen.

"My main emotion was probably one of relief," Nick Farr-Jones added.

"For me, the biggest night next to Christmas was the FA Cup. I used to wake up to watch that and I remember walking up to get the trophy from the Queen and thought of my childhood memories of FA Cup captains walking up at Wembley.

"I knew that '91 was the final throw of the dice for me, which meant a lot of pressure and a lot of build-up and speculation."

If England faced the knockout rounds on the road then Australia could claim to an even harder route to the final, first having to win in Dublin against Ireland and then needing to beat holders New Zealand, in the same city.

The Ireland game was breathtaking with the 19-18 victory being handed to the Wallabies by a last-minute try from Michael Lynagh that broke the Irish hearts. Ireland thought they had won the quarter-final minutes before with a Gordon Hamilton try.

And the semi belonged to a certain David Campese, who often used the biggest stage as his chance to shine. One sensational try against the All Blacks – and creating another for Tim Horan – Campese saw them home 16-6. "That match was magnificent from start to finish," said Farr-Jones. "In fact, the first 40 minutes was the best rugby I'd ever been involved in.

"Campo defied all the logic of the game by running across the field before sealing a superb try. And that flip over the shoulder to Tim Horan for the second try was the stuff of legend."

In contrast to England, their neighbours Wales were close to shambolic when they arrived at the World Cup, after having lost 63-6 on a tour to Australia.

And it wasn't long before Wales were presenting the rugby world with the tournament's first real shock. Wales' defeat to Western Samoa, at Cardiff.

Little of course did the Welsh know at the time but players in the Samoa team that day, including Frank Bunce, Pat Lam and Brian Lima would go on to become world stars in their own right.

Samoa had arrived at the finals as part of the first qualification tournament. The sides were invited to participate in 1987 but in 1991 eight of the 16 places were filled by the quarter-finalists from four years earlier. Thirty-two countries fought out a qualification process for the remaining eight places.

Under New Zealand coach Bryan Williams, the Samoans turned the formbook upside down beating Wales 16-13 at Cardiff Arms Park. Wales may have been pool stage casualties but Scotland – with a Grand Slam of their own in 1990 – were a powerful force in 1991, enjoying their best World Cup campaign to date.

Scotland scored 122 points in their three pool matches and after accounting for Western Samoa – 28-6 – in the quarters they faced England at Murrayfield,

BELOW David Campese scores for eventual winners, Australia, in the quarter-final against Ireland

in an epic encounter. Gavin Hastings – so often the Scotland hero – missed a straightforward penalty with the scores at 6-6, leaving Rob Andrew the chance to send England into the final.

Scotland coach Ian McGeechan was in no doubt about the key to England's win.

"England wanted to strangle the game, we wanted to keep it alive," he said.

But England manager Geoff Cooke retorted: "We would love to have cut the Scots to pieces with scintillating back play but it's not quite as easy as that."

If Scotland were unfortunate to suffer from the boot of Andrew then Ireland must still be wondering how they failed to make the semi-finals, after that heart-stopping match against eventual winners, Australia.

Canada also made a notable breakthrough, making the quarter-finals after pool stage wins over Romania and Fiji. The Canadians' tournament ended in Lille with a 29-13 defeat by New Zealand.

1991 WORLD CUP STAT ATTACK

GROUP A

N Zealand	18	England	12
Italy	30	USA	9
N Zealand	46	USA	6
England	36	Italy	6
England	37	USA	9
N Zealand	31	Italy	21

New Zealand and England qualify

GROUP B

Scotland	47	Japan	9
Ireland	55	Zimbabwe	11
Ireland	32	Japan	16
Scotland	51	Zimbabwe	12
Scotland	24	Ireland	15
Japan	52	Zimbabwe	8

Scotland and Ireland qualify

GROUP C

Australia	32	Argentina	19
Wales	13	Western Samoa	16
Australia	9	Western Samoa	3
Wales	16	Argentina	7
Australia	38	Wales	3
Argentina	12	Western Samoa	35

Australia and Western Samoa qualify

GROUP D

France	30	Romania	3
Canada	13	Fiji	3
France	33	Fiji	9
Romania	11	Canada	19
Fiji	15	Romania	17
France	19	Canada	13

France and Canada qualify

QUARTER-FINALS

Scotland	28	Western Samoa	6
France	10	England	19
Ireland	18	Australia	19
Canada	13	N Zealand	29

SEMI-FINALS

| Scotland | 6 | England | 9 |
| Australia | 16 | N Zealand | 6 |

THIRD PLACE PLAY-OFF

| N Zealand | 13 | Scotland | 6 |

WORLD CUP FINAL

| England | 6 | Australia | 12 |

1995
Uniting the Rainbow Nation

WHEN SOUTH AFRICA WERE readmitted into international rugby union in 1992 – after the sporting boycott caused by apartheid – it was pretty clear where the 1995 World Cup was going to be held. And for the first time it was to be staged in just one country.

BELOW An impressive view of the Kings Park Rugby Stadium, one of the venues for the 1995 World Cup in South Africa

The Rainbow Nation embraced the World Cup, creating a sensational tournament, which for South Africa had the perfect ending.

This Rugby World Cup was seen as the dawning of a new era, in a country where rugby meant so much. Not only was the political landscape changing but also rugby was on the very edge of the biggest change in its history, moving from an amateur sport to a professional one. Both came together in an incredible rugby tournament that captivated the world.

This World Cup went outside not only the boundaries of rugby, but of sport, as the new competition signalled the start of a new age in South Africa. A country defined for many decades by its politics was now defined by its sport.

The 1995 Rugby World Cup brought unforgettable images to the world

LEFT Jonah Lomu breaks away from the tackle of England's skipper and captain, Will Carling, on his way to scoring a try in the semi-final, 1995

over the whole competition, scoring an incredible seven tries.

Unfortunately for England four of those tries came in a semi-final that no-one will ever forget.

Before the game England captain Will Carling called Lomu "a freak" and it clearly riled the All Black into action as he was over the line with just 70 seconds gone.

What followed for England was one of the worst quarters of rugby in their history and sent the Grand Slam champions crashing out of the World Cup.

In those sensational first 20 minutes New Zealand proceeded to score three tries, kick a penalty and have No 8, Zinzan Brooke, kick a drop goal, the first ever seen by a forward in international rugby.

The All Blacks went on to win 45-29, ensuring that England – who went on to lose the third-fourth place play-off match to France – conceded more points than at any other time in their international history.

screen, from the arrival of the colossus, Jonah Lomu, to the image of South African President, Nelson Mandela handing over the Webb Ellis Cup to Springboks captain Francois Pienaar.

Mandela may have left us with the most endearing image but on the field the 1995 World Cup will be remembered for the world's first sighting of Lomu.

The 6ft 4in wing stood like a giant

South Africa had a far more conventional route into the final, beating France at rain-sodden Durban 19-15.

And it is fair to say that the final failed to live up to its billing. They are rarely classics but at least this one did make history as it became the first World Cup final to be settled in extra time.

New Zealand and South Africa were locked at 9-9 when the 80 minutes were completed, so up stepped Joel Stransky to win the game with an extra-time drop goal that sent the Rainbow Nation into raptures, with a 15-12 victory.

"No Hollywood scriptwriter could have written a better script," said Pienaar after receiving the Webb Ellis Cup from President Mandela.

"We didn't just have the support of 63,000 South Africans (in the ground) today. We had the support of 42 million South Africans (in the country).

"It was just unbelievable on the streets of South Africa. For the first time all the people had come together and all races and religions were hugging each other. It was just wonderful.

"At the final whistle I fell right to my knees. I'm a Christian and wanted to say a quick prayer for being in such a wonderful event, not because of the winning.

"Then all of a sudden I realised the whole team was around me which was a special moment."

And what about the moment when the cup was placed in your hands? "Nelson Mandela said 'thank you very much for what you've done for South Africa' but I said 'thank you for what you've done" recalled Pienaar "I almost felt like hugging him but it wasn't appropriate, I guess. Then I lifted the trophy, which was unbelievable. I can't describe the feeling as I wouldn't do it justice."

The one potentially sinister post-script came from the New Zealand team, where allegations of food poisoning surfaced, and the identity of a mystery waitress, 'Susie', who it was alleged was behind a plot to derail the

All Blacks' World Cup chances.

New Zealand coach Laurie Mains said: "It was just an amazing sequence of events and coincidence that, of our 35-man party that ate at that particular lunch venue in the hotel here, about 27 of them went down in the space of 12 hours.

"You can read what you like into that, but I don't think it was coincidence. We certainly have our suspicions."

A plot was never proved but a health problem – in the All Blacks camp – was not in doubt.

"We started falling over like flies, and that included 10 of the playing 15 and many of the other players and most of the management," added fly-half Andrew Mehrtens.

The tournament will be remembered, unfortunately, for more than the joy of the South African win as Ivory Coast wing Max Brito was paralysed after a tackle in the final Group D game against Tonga.

It was a tragic event in an otherwise joyful World Cup that for both Tonga and Ivory Coast ended with them being eliminated at the pool stage.

It was to be Ivory Coast's last appearance in a World Cup finals – to date – as

the second African place was taken by Namibia in 1999, 2003 and 2007.

The pool stages ended with a predictable quarter-final line-up, South Africa effectively taking Canada's place amongst the big boys, who were there in 1991.

Wales, after their failure to make the quarter-finals in 1991 following their defeat to Western Samoa, were forced to qualify this time around.

Wins over Romania and Italy ensured that Wales made it safely to South Africa but as a qualifier they were put in a tough group with both Ireland and New Zealand.

BELOW Tonga captain Manakaetau Otai breaks away during the match against the Ivory Coast, 1995

The All Blacks steamrollered over them and when they lost to Ireland by one point (24-23) they were destined to miss out on a place in the quarter-finals for the second successive tournament.

Western Samoa continued their development, beating Italy and Argentina for a quarter-final berth, where they lost to the host nation 42-14.

1995 WORLD CUP STAT ATTACK

GROUP A

South Africa	27	Australia	18
Canada	34	Romania	3
South Africa	21	Romania	3
Australia	27	Canada	11
Australia	42	Romania	3
South Africa	20	Canada	0

South Africa and Australia qualify

GROUP B

W Samoa	42	Italy	18
England	24	Argentina	18
W Samoa	32	Argentina	26
England	27	Italy	20
Italy	31	Argentina	25
England	44	W Samoa	22

England and Western Samoa qualify

GROUP C

Wales	57	Japan	10
N Zealand	43	Ireland	19
Ireland	50	Japan	28
N Zealand	34	Wales	9
N Zealand	145	Japan	17
Ireland	24	Wales	23

New Zealand and Ireland qualify

GROUP D

France	38	Tonga	10
Scotland	89	Ivory Coast	0
France	54	Ivory Coast	18
Scotland	41	Tonga	5
Tonga	29	Ivory Coast	11
France	22	Scotland	19

Scotland and France qualify

QUARTER-FINALS

France	36	Ireland	12
South Africa	42	W Samoa	14
England	25	Australia	22
N Zealand	48	Scotland	30

THIRD PLACE PLAY-OFF

England	9	France	19

SEMI-FINALS

South Africa	19	France	15
N Zealand	45	England	29

WORLD CUP **FINAL**

South Africa	15	N Zealand	12

1999
Wallabies clinch the double

THE QUALIFICATION PROCEDURES for the third World Cup were revamped with only the champions (South Africa), the runners-up (New Zealand) and the third place play-off winners (France) from 1995 going through as of right.

This forced giants like England into a qualification tournament, where they ran into Holland and Italy.

The qualification process didn't make a huge difference to the sides that made it through to the finals, although with 20 teams (up from 16) reaching the finals we saw tournament debuts for Spain, Uruguay and Namibia.

Uruguay won their 'minnows World Cup' with a 27-15 win over Spain in the first game, Uruguayan flanker Diego Ormaechea, becoming the oldest man – at 40 – to play in a match at the World Cup finals.

After a sensational tournament in 1995, the World Cup organisers unfortunately erred on a number of issues for this tournament and it certainly did not surpass the competition in South Africa.

RIGHT Diego Ormaechea of Uruguay scored his country's first try in the tournament to set them on the road to a 27-15 victory against Spain in 1999

Wales were the hosts but the biggest problem was in allowing matches to also be staged in Paris, Glasgow, Edinburgh, Twickenham, Dublin, Lens, Bordeaux, Huddersfield, Bristol, Toulouse, Beziers, Leicester, Limerick, Belfast and Galshiels.

Had the World Cup organisers learnt nothing from 1995 where the success was based around the tournament taking place in one nation? The marketing and promotion of the 1999 World Cup was a mess, and too many games were played in front of half-empty stadiums.

The increase in the number of teams to 20 was welcomed but the decision to divide those 20 teams into five pools of four teams was not.

While it meant one less pool match, the new system ensured the installation of a quarter-final play-off for six sides that failed to win their group. The games in the quarter-final play-off round were hopelessly timed shortly after the final pool match and too close to the actual quarter-finals.

The play-off system did allow Argentina to make a significant breakthrough and make their first quarter-final, after a victory over Ireland in Lens.

Gonzalo Quesada, who finished this World Cup as the leading scorer, was the hero with seven penalties and a conversion after Diego Albanese's late try.

The Pumas couldn't keep their run going in the last eight, losing 47-26 to France.

In any other World Cup, England would have moved into the quarter-finals by finishing second in their pool but in 1999 that was only good enough for a play-off against Fiji.

ABOVE English fullback Matt Perry (left) collides with New Zealand winger Jonah Lomu during the first-round match, 1999 away and I thought it was his day."

In truth, although England were knocked out by the South Africans, 44-21, it was their pool match defeat by New Zealand that actually destined them to an early exit.

Against New Zealand it was once again Jonah Lomu who came to haunt them, as the giant wing scored a 50-metre try, blasting through the English defence, as the All Blacks won 30-16. They couldn't hold Lomu in 1995 and it was the same story four years later.

That victory over England and a subsequent hammering of Scotland in the quarter-finals sent New Zealand into the last four as the hot favourites to claim their second world title.

But the All Blacks hadn't bargained for the unpredictability of the French, who staged the greatest comeback in World Cup history, to win 43-31.

In a semi-final played at Twickenham, France looked down and out when they went 24-10 behind to a side in magnificent form but upsetting the odds the French managed to score 33 points, with only seven from the All Blacks, to storm home.

"We let ourselves and our fans down and we are quite devastated,"

The fact that England won easily, 45-24, did little for their preparations for the last-eight clash with South Africa – in Paris – as it followed four days later. In that match Springbok fly-half Jannie De Beer kicked a world record five drop goals to help send England out.

"Jannie's was a truly phenomenal performance," said South Africa coach Nick Mallett.

"I told him before the game 'go out and have a bash'. He stuck one or two said New Zealand coach John Hart, who subsequently lost his job. "The coach is accountable and I take full responsibility.

"We are a young side but that's no excuse. At 24-10, no way we should have lost."

In the other semi-final Stephen Larkham took Australia into the final with a dramatic drop-goal winner that stunned opponents South Africa, Matt Burke finishing them off with a late penalty.

"Stephen Larkham produced a wonder drop goal. When he did that there was pure elation, well on my behalf anyway, followed by a realisation we had to get back to it," said captain John Eales of the extra time victory.

"They were set to get right back out at us. But we managed to hold them off."

Australia duly won their second World Cup with a final 35-12 victory over France, at a tournament when defence was king. Australia in fact only conceded one try in the whole competition and that to a USA side – in a group game – after it was clear they were going to win.

"Straight after the game I turned to anyone who was there just to celebrate and go crazy," Eales added on BBC online.

"And then I realised I was going to get the trophy from the Queen. I thought "better make sure you don't swear" and after that was just really excited to represent the team and Australian rugby.

"I was filled with an immense satisfaction that we had achieved what we wanted to do – goals which had been set by some of us four years ago."

BELOW Stephen Larkham of Australia kicks a 40m drop-goal during the semi-final of the 1999 World Cup against South Africa

1999 WORLD CUP STAT ATTACK

GROUP A

Spain	15	Uruguay	27
Scotland	29	South Africa	46
Scotland	43	Uruguay	12
South Africa	47	Spain	3
South Africa	39	Uruguay	3
Scotland	48	Spain	0

South Africa and Scotland qualify

GROUP B

England	67	Italy	7
New Zealand	45	Tonga	9
England	16	New Zealand	30
Italy	25	Tonga	28
New Zealand	101	Italy	3
England	101	Tonga	10

England and New Zealand qualify

GROUP C

Fiji	67	Namibia	18
France	33	Canada	20
France	47	Namibia	13
Fiji	38	Canada	22
Canada	72	Namibia	11
France	28	Fiji	19

France and Fiji qualify

GROUP D

Wales	23	Argentina	18
Samoa	43	Japan	9
Wales	64	Japan	15
Argentina	32	Samoa	16
Wales	31	Samoa	38
Argentina	33	Japan	12

Wales and Argentina qualify

GROUP E

Ireland	53	USA	8
Australia	57	Romania	9
USA	25	Romania	27
Ireland	3	Australia	23
Australia	55	USA	19
Ireland	44	Romania	14

Australia and Ireland qualify

QUARTER-FINAL PLAY-OFFS

Scotland	35	Samoa	20
England	45	Fiji	24
Argentina	28	Ireland	24

QUARTER-FINALS

Wales	9	Australia	24
England	21	South Africa	44
Scotland	18	New Zealand	30
Argentina	26	France	47

SEMI-FINALS

Australia	27	South Africa	21
France	43	New Zealand	31

THIRD PLACE PLAY-OFF

New Zealand	18	South Africa	22

WORLD CUP FINAL

Australia	35	France	12

2003
Jonny gets England home

IT ONLY TOOK 16 YEARS, BUT finally – in 2003 – a side from the northern hemisphere won the Webb Ellis Cup: Clive Woodward's England.

The victory came in the most dramatic of styles. England and Australia locked together through 80 minutes of action and for a further 18 minutes of extra time they were separated only by an unforgettable drop goal by Jonny Wilkinson

Nine points behind at half-time, the Wallabies valiantly fought back through the boot of Elton Flatley to force extra time, before Wilkinson had the final word.

"It was a huge effort by the entire squad of players, coaches and backroom staff, everybody. Thanks to the fans, they were incredible," said England captain Martin Johnson.

"I can't say enough about the team,

RIGHT Nathan Sharpe charges through the Irish lines but his Australia side came up short in their attempt to retain the World Cup

OPPOSITE Wales' great performance against New Zealand in the group stages restored the belief in their abilities

because we had the lead and we lost it but we came back. And I can't say enough about Wilko at the end.

"I'm just happy for the players, they've put their heart and soul into it. It couldn't have been any closer and I'm just happy I'm on the right side."

Wilkinson was typically modest refusing – as usual – to take any praise despite winning it with that drop goal, scored with his weaker right foot.

"It was a massive team effort and a huge feeling of togetherness we had, certainly for the rest of the evening and through today as well," Wilkinson said. "It was an amazing feeling." Australia captain, George Gregan, was at his dignified best at the end, as he realised neither side could have done any more on a wonderful day for rugby.

"Congratulations must be extended to the English team, they delivered under pressure and they delivered when it counted," Gregan said.

"But I'm so proud of my guys. We gutsed it out, we fought back, we were down 14-5, we brought it back to extra-time." Woodward was the mastermind behind the victory and when he returned to England he was soon knighted.

From the moment England exited the 1999 tournament Woodward started a root and branch review of the England team, bringing in a plethora of specialist coaches and developing his team with a philosophy of trying to do 100 things one per cent better.

It was also a tournament when two former world champions – New Zealand and South Africa – imploded in public.

New Zealand disappointed their legions of fans by losing their semi-final against Australia, under the coaching of John Mitchell, who paid for the failure with his job.

If the fall out was bad in New Zealand it was even worse in South Africa, where their quarter-final exit was the subject of ministerial questions.

The Springboks were beaten by England in the group stages and eventually lost 29-9 to New Zealand in the last eight, the first World Cup when they hadn't managed to make at least the semi-finals.

Not only did the Boks suffer on the pitch but off it as well as a video of naked players at their pre-World Cup training camp was shown around the world.

"This was apartheid-style military training and was dehumanising for the players," said South Africa's sports minister Ngconde Balfour. "In discussion with the SARFU president I have expressed my total condemnation and disgust at elements of the camp."

After suffering in the 1990s, Wales continued their re-emergence on the World Cup stage, coming closest to knocking England out in a memorable quarter-final in Brisbane.

Wales led 10-3, three minutes into the second half, before Will Greenwood inspired an England comeback with a try, and Woodward's team never looked back.

"We're gutted we couldn't get up but we've come a long way and I can't say any more than that," Wales coach Steve Hansen said, after seeing his side outscore England three tries to one.

Wales had got their belief from a 53-37 defeat to New Zealand that saw them outgun the All Blacks for long periods, even leading 37-33 at the start of the second half.

"We've raised our performances week

by week but this was one hurdle we couldn't get over and the guys are very disappointed with the result," said Wales captain Colin Charvis, after the defeat to England.

"We thought we had a good chance – especially going in at half-time – but unfortunately England were a bit too strong for us." Unfortunately for the sides outside the world's top 12 – and those who value the promotion of rugby as a global game – it was a World Cup that polarised the nations at the top and bottom of the rankings.

England hammered Uruguay 111-13 and Australia went a step further with a record score in the finals, beating Namibia 142-0.

The Wallabies ran in a record 22 tries, which did the World Cup little good. Twenty-four hours before, New Zealand had surpassed Australia's previous tournament record score with a 91-7 victory over Tonga.

The number of huge scores led to a predictable quarter-final line-up, Fiji coming closest to breaking into the party, although they fell to Scotland, 22-20, in the group decider.

The Fijians did uncover one world star in the almost unstoppable Rupeni Caucaunibuca. He scored two tries in the game against Scotland but Tom Smith's score two minutes from time sent the Scots through.

With stars like Caucaunibuca, Wilkinson and Gregan on parade, the 2003 tournament was hailed as the best

BELOW Jonny Wilkinson was England's hero in the final, kicking a last-minute drop goal to win the World Cup

ever, with almost two million spectators – in ten cities – going through the turnstiles, to watch the 48 games, across 44 days.

More than 40,000 overseas visitors arrived in Australia for the tournament as once again the organisers decided to stage the World Cup in just one country.

But what made the tournament so special was the way it was embraced by the Australian people, who not only flocked to the big games but ensured there was a great atmosphere at the small clashes, like when Romania took on Namibia in Launceston.

"We were absolutely delighted with it. It has taken it to a new level," said Syd Millar, chairman of the International Rugby Board.

2003 WORLD CUP STAT ATTACK

GROUP A

Australia	24	Argentina	8
Ireland	45	Romania	17
Argentina	67	Namibia	14
Australia	90	Romania	8
Ireland	64	Namibia	7
Argentina	50	Romania	3
Australia	142	Namibia	0
Argentina	15	Ireland	16
Namibia	7	Romania	37
Australia	17	Ireland	16

Australia and Ireland qualify

GROUP B

France	61	Fiji	18
Scotland	32	Japan	11
Fiji	19	USA	18
France	51	Japan	29
Scotland	39	USA	15
Fiji	41	Japan	13
France	51	Scotland	9
Japan	26	USA	39
France	41	USA	14
Scotland	22	Fiji	20

France and Scotland qualify

GROUP C

South Africa	72	Uruguay	6
England	84	Georgia	6
Samoa	60	Uruguay	13
South Africa	6	England	25
Georgia	9	Samoa	46
South Africa	46	Georgia	19
Samoa	22	England	35
Georgia	12	Uruguay	24
South Africa	60	Samoa	10
England	111	Uruguay	13

England and South Africa qualify

GROUP D

N Zealand	70	Italy	7
Wales	41	Canada	10
Italy	36	Tonga	12
N Zealand	68	Canada	6
Tonga	20	Wales	27
Canada	14	Italy	19
N Zealand	91	Tonga	7
Italy	15	Wales	27
Canada	24	Tonga	7
N Zealand	53	Wales	37

New Zealand and Wales qualify

QUARTER-FINALS

N Zealand	29	South Africa	9
Australia	33	Scotland	16
France	43	Ireland	21
England	28	Wales	17

SEMI-FINALS

| N Zealand | 10 | Australia | 22 |
| England | 24 | France | 7 |

THIRD PLACE PLAY-OFF

| France | 13 | N Zealand | 40 |

WORLD CUP **FINAL**

| Australia | 17 | England | 20 |

2007
England back in the Final

THE ENGLISH SIDE THAT HAD won the 2003 World Cup immediately broke up as its stars retired or succumbed to long-term injury, so it was something of a surprise when a new-look team battled its way to consecutive finals in 2007. They struggled against the United States in their pool match before being humbled by South Africa (36-0), but they recovered to beat Samoa and Tonga and eventually finished second in the group.

There were few surprises as South Africa won all four matches easily and topped the pool. Saamoa underperformed and allowed Tonga to take third place, which left the USA bottom of the group without a win.

Wales were drawn alongside Canada, Japan, Australia and Fiji in Pool B. They beat Canada convincingly but lost to Australia by 12 points in Cardiff. They then thumped Japan but still had to win

their final pool game against a Fijian side that played an exciting brand of rugby. What followed was perhaps the greatest game ever played.

The Welsh started fast and Shane Williams almost scored in the second minute after a length-of-the-field move. After 15 minutes, the Fijian pack rum-

RIGHT The Opening Ceremony 2007

OPPOSITE England fans in good spirit before the game with Samao, 2007 Rugby World Cup bled forwards and Nicky Little converted Akapusi Qera's try under the posts. Fiji ran the ball from the restart and Vilimoni Delasau collected his own chip to score a magnificent solo effort. Although Little couldn't add the conversion, he then kicked a penalty to give Fiji a 15-3 lead. He added another two minutes later and Fiji scored a superb third try through Kele Leawere. The islanders were almost out of sight after only a quarter of the game.

The Welsh responded by hammering the Fijian defence. Alix Popham touched down after a scrum and James Hook added the conversion but Fiji maintained a 15-point lead at half-time. Shane Williams then scored a magnificent solo try, sidestepping three defenders and racing in from 80 metres. Hook added the conversion and the Welsh were within eight. Another superb backline move saw Gareth Thomas score to mark his 100th cap. Jones struck the post with the conversion so Fiji retained a three-point lead. A slick lineout move then saw Mark Jones scoring a super try in the opposite corner, and the Welsh appeared to have completed a miraculous comeback when Jones added the extras.

Little pegged the Welsh back with a penalty, however, and then restored the Fijian lead with another after an hour. The game turned again when Martyn Williams intercepted a pass with seven minutes to go and ran 60 metres to score. Stephen Jones hit the post for the third time with the conversion. With only four minutes left, Graham Dewes scored from close range and Little added the conversion to give Fiji a four-point advantage. It was a lead they maintained in the face of unrelenting Welsh pressure.

Fiji and Australia therefore qualified from Pool B, while New Zealand and Scotland went through from Pool C. The All Blacks thrashed Italy, Portugal, Scotland and Romania by an average of 75 points, so the only match of consequence in the group was Italy against Scotland as this decided who would finish second and qualify alongside the Kiwis. It was a dour game that was won by the boot of Chris Paterson.

In Pool D, Argentina caused an upset

BELOW Denis Hickie during Ireland's close encouter with Georgia at the 2007 Rugby World Cup by beating hosts France in their opening match in the Stade de France. The French had been expected to qualify easily but their fans turned on the team as the Pumas edged a tight game by five points. France recovered to beat a very disappointing Ireland side that had struggled against minnows Namibia and then almost lost to lowly Georgia. Argentina built on their solid start and topped the group after remaining unbeaten. France joined them after a comfortable win over Georgia in their final group game.

England were expected to be trounced by Australia in the first quarter-final but the English defence was magnificent and a fit-again Wilkinson kicked the decisive points. New Zealand then choked once more as France overhauled them to win an epic game in Cardiff. Dan Carter had given the All Blacks the lead with a penalty and then Luke McAlister added a try three min-

BELOW South Africa cross the line during their 36-0 victory over England in Group A

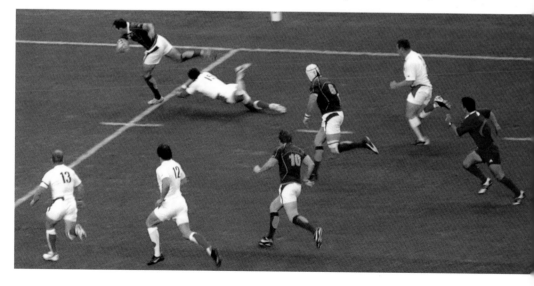

utes later. Carter kicked another penalty and it took until the last minute of the half before France replied with a three-pointer of their own. Both sides added tries before Yannick Jauzion crossed the New Zealand line for the crucial score 10 minutes from the end.

South Africa and Argentina beat Fiji and Scotland respectively. England somehow overcame the French in Paris in a tight semi-final, while South Africa continued their march to the final with an easy win over Argentina. With the memory of their pool-stage drubbing still fresh in the mind, England seemed a little flat in the final and South Africa won the tournament for the second time with a 15-6 victory. More than two million tickets were sold for the 48 matches.

2007 WORLD CUP STAT ATTACK

GROUP A

England	44	Samoa	22
England	0	South Africa	36
England	36	Tonga	20
England	28	USA	10
Samoa	7	South Africa	59
Samoa	15	Tonga	19
Samoa	25	USA	21
South Africa	30	Tonga	25
South Africa	64	USA	15
Tonga	25	USA	15

South Africa and England qualify

GROUP B

Australia	37	Canada	6
Australia	55	Fiji	12
Australia	91	Japan	3
Australia	32	Wales	20
Canada	16	Fiji	29
Canada	12	Japan	12
Canada	17	Wales	42
Fiji	35	Japan	31
Fiji	38	Wales	34
Japan	18	Wales	72

Australia and Fiji qualify

GROUP C

Italy	14	N Zealand	76
Italy	31	Portugal	76
Italy	24	Romania	18
Italy	16	Scotland	18
N Zealand	108	Portugal	13
N Zealand	85	Romania	8
N Zealand	40	Scotland	0
Portugal	10	Romania	14
Portugal	10	Scotland	56
Romania	0	Scotland	42

New Zealand and Scotland qualify

GROUP D

Argentina	17	France	12
Argentina	33	Georgia	3
Argentina	30	Ireland	15
Agentina	63	Namibia	3
France	64	Georgia	7
France	25	Ireland	3
France	87	Namabia	10
Georgia	10	Ireland	14
Georgia	30	Namibia	0
Ireland	32	Namibia	17

Argentina and France qualify

QUARTER-FINALS

Australia	10	England	12
New Zealand	18	France	20
South Africa	37	Fiji	20
Argentina	19	Scotland	13

SEMI-FINALS

England	14	France	9
South Africa	37	Argentina	13

THIRD PLACE PLAY-OFF

France	10	Argentina	34

WORLD CUP **FINAL**

England	6	South Africa	15

2011
The All Blacks are Back

NEW ZEALAND BEAT STRONG BIDS from South Africa and Japan for the right to host the seventh World Cup, and the home side was determined to exorcise the ghosts of previous failures. Never has the pressure on the favourites been so intense, so palpable. Organisers also found themselves under pressure to redevelop outdated stadia but, come September 2011, the country was ready.

The qualifying tournament had been expanded to 91 teams but the finals themselves saw 20 sides split into four groups. The hosts beat France 37-17 in Auckland but both sides qualified from Pool A even though the French suffered a shocking 19-14 defeat to Tonga in Wellington.

England and Argentina topped their group at the expense of Scotland, while in Pool C Ireland finally registered a win over Australia, the side that had so often been their nemesis. Both went through

to the quarter-finals and consigned a promising Italian side to third place. South Africa and Wales rounded out the last eight after overcoming heavy resistance from Samoa. The brutal top-of-the-table clash between the Welsh and the defending champions in Wellington went down to the wire but a late Francois Hougaard try won the match for South Africa.

The quarter-finals were all low-scoring affairs with only New Zealand progressing comfortably after a 33-10 win over Argentina. A resurgent Wales finally lived up to expectation with a 22-10 victory against Ireland. England had been in the international wilderness after their heroics in 2007 and were edged out by France, and then Australia squeezed past South Africa.

The first semi-final was another tight encounter that Wales should have won. Captain Sam Warburton was sent off by Alain Rolland for a dangerous tackle only 18 minutes into the game but the Welsh refused to change their attacking philosophy and, had James Hook not missed two penalties, Stephen Jones's conversion not hit the post and Leigh Halfpenny's last-minute penalty from 45 metres not fallen inches short, they rather than a lacklustre France would have made the final.

New Zealand lived up to their

BELOW Australia vs USA, Rugby World Cup 2011

BELOW France vs Tonga, Rugby World Cup 2011

OPPOSITE South Africa vs Fiji, Rugby World Cup 2011

favourites billing by beating Australia 20-6 in the second semi-final, but they almost choked again in the final. The French had broken their hearts twice before (the 1999 defeat at Twickenham was etched on the public consciousness and the capitulation in the last minutes of the 2007 quarter-final sent a nation into mourning) but this time the All Blacks held on to win their first World Cup since the inaugural tournament putting their 24-year nightmare behind them as they beat France 8-7 in the lowest scoring Rugby World Cup final ever.

When captain Richie McCaw raised the Webb Ellis Cup, the capacity Eden Park crowd of 61,000 - and a nation of four million supporters - bellowed their adoration and breathed a collective sigh of relief.

The torment which had followed the All Blacks for the past five tournaments had been erased and the team – coached by Graham Henry – proved they were worthy winners and the best team of the tournament.

The game was no push over though. France came to play, and made their intentions clear just before kick

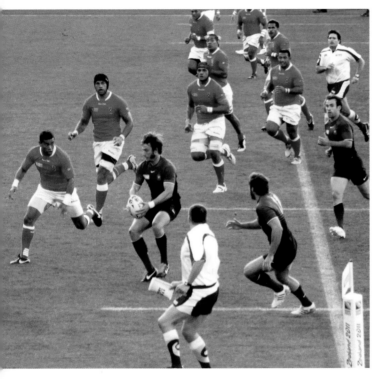

off as they challenged the Haka in a unique and somewhat controversial way.

Wearing their white away strip, France linked arms and formed a 'flying V' before marching menacingly towards the All Blacks, making it clear they weren't going to simply make up the numbers in this their third RWC final.

"I wasn't alone, I had my teammates with me. I felt them close to me — too close at one stage, because they wanted to go across the field and hug New Zealand," said captain Thierry Dusautoir.

"It was necessary to calm them down. But it's a great moment that we'll all remember. I felt during the week that the players wanted to do something during the haka, like they did in 2007. "

Prop Fabien Barcella was one of the Frenchman who continued forward, having to be held back at times. "It was a 'V' for victory, quite simply. It was the chance of a lifetime to play a final at Eden Park, we didn't want to miss out on it. It came from the heart, and showed that the 30 of us were together that night."

Francois Trinh-Duc, the fly-half who started off of the bench, said that the players needed to make an impression on their opponents: "We had to throw down the challenge to them. It was a way of defying them, letting them know we were there. I think they were surprised, they weren't expecting it. "

Indeed, France gave them a greater scare than anyone imagined. Similar to the sides' pool match, the French held possession for large chunks of the opening period until Piri Weepu made a significant impact.

He won a turnover penalty and then kicked 50 metres downfield to a lineout where the All Blacks pulled out a piece of practice-ground magic. Keven Mealamu lobbed the delivery to the back where Jerome Kaino passed it down to Tony Woodcock who charged over the try-line.

Weepu missed the conversion and all three of his attempts in the opening half which left the All Blacks without much of a buffer at the break.

The French had their troubles too: Morgan Parra was battered by a Ma'a

Nonu charge which signalled his exit from the test after 22 minutes.

Kieran Read was piling on the pressure for the French with his charging runs in midfield, breaking the advantage line with every foray and giving Weepu options either side of the rucks.

The French clung on resolutely, trusting their defence would hold and they could ride out the assaults. After half an hour they hadn't conceded any more points and began to string several phases together.

They also watched the All Blacks lose Aaron Cruden to injury when he was sandwiched in a double tackle and hyper-extended his right knee.

His misfortune brought Stephen Donald on to the park, a squad replacement and the fourth-choice pivot making his first tournament appearance in the World Cup final.

The tension was palpable in the stadium and it was spreading to the players at the break. There was some respite when Donald took over the kicking duties and landed a 36 metre penalty but the French were not done.

Weepu made a careless hack at a loose ball from the base of a ruck and only succeeded in chipping it into the hands of replacement five-eighths Francois Trinh-Duc.

He weaved downfield and with Aurelien Rougerie in support, France worked their way towards the line and, the defence outflanked, captain Thierry Dusautoir strolled across.

Trinh-Duc kicked the conversion and the All Black selectors sent Weepu and Sam Whitelock to the cooler.

Thirty minutes were left, France had the momentum and somehow the All Blacks had to find an antidote. They struggled.

Trinh-Duc missed a 48 metre penalty but France pushed on. Israel Dagg lost the ball in a mid-air leap near his 22 and Andy Ellis's kick was charged down.

The All Blacks needed to play territory. Dagg found some with a deep kick then Donald squeezed a smart kick downfield. But France countered with their lineout where they had at least five jumpers and dominated the air.

Ten minutes left and France still came forward. The All Blacks used all their defensive clout to repel them. Who would crack in the brutality? Not the All Blacks; not this time.

Eventually referee Craig Joubert stilled their nerves and those of the whole country when he signalled the end of a chilling contest.

The 2011 All Blacks were the World Cup winners, champions of the world, the elite class to stand alongside their 1987 predecessors.

A nation was finally released from its torment. Wales played their part in an entertaining bronze-medal match against Australia but the Wallabies won 21-18.

2011 WORLD CUP STAT ATTACK

GROUP A

N Zealand	41	Tonga	10
France	47	Japan	21
Tonga	20	Canada	25
N Zealand	83	Japan	7
France	46	Canada	19
Tonga	31	Japan	18
N Zealand	37	France	17
Canada	23	Japan	23
France	14	Tonga	19
N Zealand	79	Canada	15

New Zealand and France qualify

GROUP B

Scotland	34	Romania	24
England	13	Argentina	9
Scotland	15	Georgia	6
Argentina	43	Romania	8
England	41	Georgia	10
England	67	Romania	3
Argentina	13	Scotland	12
Georgia	25	Romania	9
England	16	Scotland	12
Argentina	25	Georgia	7

England and Argentina qualify

GROUP C

Australia	32	Italy	6
Ireland	22	USA	10
Russia	6	USA	13
Australia	6	Ireland	15
Italy	53	Russia	17
Australia	67	USA	5
Ireland	62	Russia	12
Italy	27	USA	10
Australia	68	Russia	22
Ireland	36	Italy	6

Ireland and Australia qualify

GROUP D

Fiji	49	Namibia	25
South Africa	17	Wales	16
Samoa	49	Namibia	12
South Africa	49	Fiji	3
Wales	17	Samoa	10
South Africa	87	Namibia	0
Fiji	7	Samoa	27
Wales	81	Namibia	7
South Africa	13	Samoa	5
Wales	66	Fiji	0

South Africa and wales qualify

QUARTER-FINALS

Ireland	10	Wales	22
England	12	France	19
South Africa	9	Australia	11
N Zealand	33	Argentina	10

SEMI-FINALS

Wales	8	France	9
Australia	6	N Zealand	20

THIRD PLACE PLAY-OFF

Wales	18	Australia	21

WORLD CUP FINAL

France	7	N Zealand	8

Chapter 3

A – Z of the Rugby World Cup

A – Australia

BELOW Australian players pose with the trophy after the 1999 final game

THE COUNTRY WITH THE SECOND most successful World Cup record – despite having one of the smallest playing bases – have won the Webb Ellis Cup twice, in 1991 and 1999, a feat subsequently equalled by New Zealand.

After losing a very disappointing third-fourth play-off in 1987, Australia certainly didn't arrive at the 1991 tournament as one of the favourites. But they still had the nucleus of their 1984 Grand Slam side, and used that as their key to victory. The seminal game in 1991 came in the quarter-final when they looked down and out – in Dublin – after Gordon Hamilton scored a late try, which looked to have won the game. But stand-in captain Michael Lynagh replied with a length of the field move that took Australia into the semis. "That game – against Ireland - was the most emotional time of my life," remembered Australia captain Nick Farr-Jones. "It was similar to the birth of one of my children crammed into about four minutes.

"I'd like to think had I been on the field we wouldn't have been in that won in the dying seconds by a Rob Andrew drop goal but in 1999 with a new generation of players in the side they dominated the tournament, conceding just one try, and that was against the USA – in a pool game – when they had rested the majority of their front-line players. The final victory was the biggest in World Cup history with Australia trouncing the French 35-12.

It was the tournament where defence ruled the world, the Wallabies' almost watertight last line winning the day.

"The All Blacks were the favourites, the Springboks were defending champions and England were the great local hope," said Australia captain John Eales.

"As it turned out none of those teams made the final - it was us, and our mental focus had to be really strong. I was filled with an immense satisfaction that we had achieved what we wanted to do - goals which had been set by some of us four years ago."

Australia failed to become the first side to retain the Webb Ellis Cup. On home soil – in 2003 – they lost in extra time to a last-gasp drop goal from Jonny Wilkinson. They faced a stiff test to get out of the group stage in 2015 as their pool also included England and Wales.

LEFT Nick Farr-Jones lifts the Rugby World Cup after their victory in the 1991 World Cup final

position but when Gordon Hamilton scored, Michael Lynagh treated the situation very differently to how I would.

"I would have read the riot act but Michael asked the ref how long was left and then said he would kick long. That took guts and the rest is history as he went on to score. For sure we were lucky. One minute we were down and out of the World Cup and the next we were somehow back in it and on our way to face New Zealand."

Australia crashed out in the 1995 World Cup to England in a quarter-final

B – Derek Bevan

THE REFEREE FROM CLYDACH, Derek Bevan, is part of an elite band of officials to take charge of a Rugby World Cup final, standing in the middle in 1991 as Australia beat England.

In 1995 Bevan was presented with a gold watch by South African president Louis Luyt at the end of the tournament as the best referee, even though Ed Morrison officiated in the final. Bevan was referee in South Africa's semi-final win over France.

Bevan was under huge pressure in that semi-final as a deluge meant the game was delayed 90 minutes and some thought it should have been delayed 24 hours, which would have caused huge problems for the World Cup organisers.

Bevan – who took up refereeing aged 25, after playing for Vardre - was among 17 Welsh International officials who received a traditional rugby 'cap' to mark their Test status at a special ceremony at the Millennium Stadium in 2006. By the end of the 2005-06 season there had been 54 referees from Wales who had controlled international matches and Bevan still holds the world record for the number of Tests he blew in – 44, over 15 years.

When Bevan – an electrical training officer - retired in 2000 he'd spent 26 years as a referee.

His last Test match was Ireland against Italy at Lansdowne Road.

"Derek quickly appreciated that the modern game demands a high level of fitness from all participants, including referees, so he changed his diet and upped his fitness training," said fellow Welsh referee Clive Norling.

"I know some people will find it hard to believe that referees also make friends but I regard that as the biggest bonus from doing something I have always enjoyed, with the good times far outweighing the bad," Bevan added.

The full line-up of World Cup Final referees.

Year	Referee
1987	Kerry Fitzgerald (Australia)
1991	Derek Bevan (Wales)
1995	Ed Morrison (England)
1999	Andre Watson (South Africa)
2003	Andre Watson (South Africa)
2007	Alain Rolland (Ireland)
2011	Craig Joubert (South Africa)

C – Canada

ONE OF THE SIDES HURT MOST BY the advent of professionalism, Canada made a memorable World Cup quarter-final while the game was still amateur, in 1991. Victories over Romania and Fiji and only a six-point defeat to France, sent the Canadians through, where they were unfortunate to be paired with holders New Zealand, losing 29-13, in Lille, even though they outscored the All Blacks 10-8 in the second half. "'We decided to do a lap of honour to say thanks to the French people who have given us such wonderful support here," recalled Canada captain Mark Wyatt.

Canada's hopes of following up their last eighth place in 1991 with another one in 1995 were almost extinguished by the draw. Not only were they placed in the same group as hosts – and one of the favourites – South Africa but with the holders, Australia. Canada in fact came very close to upsetting South Africa in an explosive final group match, where victory would have sent the Canadians through. The game boiled over with two Canadians – Rod Snow and Gareth Rees – and one South Africa – James Dalton – sent off following a brawl as Canada crashed out under a 20-0 defeat. They were also eliminated in the Pool Stages in 2007 and 2011.

BELOW Canada made the quarter-finals in 1991, losing to New Zealand

D – Jannie de Beer

ENGLAND WENT INTO THE 1999 World Cup quarter-final, against South Africa, as the underdogs. South Africa were the holders and England had been forced into a quarter-final play-off match four days before. Pundits expected them to lose but no one predicted the way they would lose, going out to a record-breaking feat from Springboks fly-half Jannie de Beer. The South African No 10 kicked an incredible five drop goals – in a 34-point haul - at the Stade de France. Far and away a world record. No side in the history of the World Cup had played with such a game plan, using the drop goal as their most potent weapon. De Beer was the executioner as the Springboks – and particularly centre Pieter Muller – worked themselves into positions to give their outside-half the chances he needed. "There was something supernatural happening out there, I definitely believe that," De Beer said. "I believe in my heart that victory was not just about the efforts of the players. I feel God had a hand in this.

"I want to give him the glory. It was he who gave us the talent. You can plan up to a point, but there are just some things that happen that you don't have answers for.

"Some of the things that happened on that pitch I don't have answers for. I gave my heart to the Lord in '93 and ever since that time, whenever I do anything, it's to glorify him.

"I have an individual relationship with Jesus Christ. I know he is my saviour and if things happen to me it's not by coincidence or because of my own brilliance.

"You can win a World Cup but if you don't have Jesus Christ you don't have anything."

De Beer failed to continue his incredible form into the semi-finals where – ironically – Stephen Larkham booted a drop goal to put Australia into the final, and knock South Africa out.

"I made a prediction that he would get three drop goals but I didn't expect five," said South Africa coach Nick Mallett.

"When somebody doesn't miss a kick all game and gets five out of five drop goals it's a special performance.

"You can't defend against drop goals," Woodward added. "I have never seen five drop goals in a game, especially one of this importance."

BELOW Jannie de Beer kicks his fourth drop goal against England in a quarter-final match, 1999

E – Eden Park

EDEN PARK, IN AUCKLAND, New Zealand, became the first stadium to host two Rugby World Cup Finals in 2011, having previously held the inaugural final in 1987.

Situated on the boundary between the suburbs of Mount Eden and Kingsland, its rich sporting and social history and its international profile are unmatched by any other stadium in the country.

Although used primarily for rugby union in winter and cricket in summer (it hosted a number of key matches in the 2015 Cricket World Cup) the 50,000-seater stadium has also hosted the Rugby League World Cup Final in 1988, giving the venue the distinction of hosting the Union and League World Cup Finals in consecutive years,

At the Rugby World Cup in 2011 it hosted pool games, two quarter-finals, both semi-finals and the final. By amazing coincidence, the four teams that

reached the semi-finals in 2011 were the same teams that reached the semi-finals in 1987, and the third-place and final matches consisted of the same national teams as in 1987; New Zealand won both tournaments on home soil.

Like many national stadiums, Eden Park also hosts myriad other sports and in 2015 alone was the venue for the Bledisloe Cup, ITM Cup, Super Rugby, Georgie Pie Super Smash, Wellington Phoenix Football and Dick Smith NRL Auckland Nines games.

ABOVE An aerial view of Eden Park which hosted the biggest games of the 2011 World Cup

F – France

OF ALL THE NORTHERN HEMI-SPHERE hemisphere teams, France is the most successful having been runners-up on three occasions (in 1987, 1999 and 2011), third (in 1995) and fourth (in 2003 and 2007). Their affinity with the competition is reflected in the fact that they have staged pool matches in two tournaments, in 1991 and 1999, and they hosted the tournament in 2007 (although some group matches were played in Wales and Scotland) with the final being staged at the magnificent Stade de France. Their best performance was in 1987 when they reached their first final with players like Serge Blanco, Philippe Sella and Didier Camberabero in their pomp. At that tournament they beat Australia 30-24 in the semi final, coming from behind three times, the final time a try from Blanco going down in history as one of the best in World Cup history.

France staged one of the biggest shocks in World Cup history in 1999 when they upset hot favourites New Zealand – at Twickenham – in the semi-final. In an unforgettable game France slipped 24-10 behind but then proceeded to score 33 points to seven from the All Blacks, in a display that summed up everything good about French rugby. "France's stunning win over the All Blacks was the sporting equivalent of the Titanic getting the better of the iceberg, the sledgehammer losing to the nut," exclaimed Rob Kitson in The Guardian. "For a World Cup in danger of toppling off its narrow ridge on the cliff-face of international affairs, it was almost too good to be true. When Bill McLaren describes Sunday's spectacular as the greatest game of rugby he has ever seen, there can be simply no doubting France's achievement."

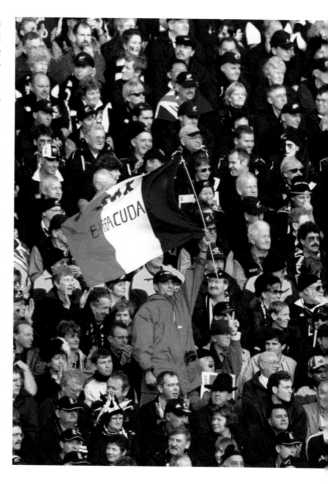

G – Georgia

AFTER RUGBY TURNED PROFESSIONAL in 1995 great efforts were made to ensure it wasn't a case of the rich (unions) getting richer and the poor unions getting poorer. So it was with great joy across the rugby world when Georgia emerged from Europe to qualify for the 2003 World Cup.

Their qualification was a massive spectacle in Georgia with 45,000 people converging on the National Stadium with around one and half million people watching the match live on national television, as they beat Russia to go through.

The draw wasn't too kind to them, though as they were placed in the same group as England and South Africa.

But it was about the experience for the likeable Georgians. "We can say the Georgian baby was born in Australia because in World Cup history whenever we take part in the future the media

BELOW Georgia players line up before the Rugby World Cup qualifier against Portugal, November 2006

guides will say 'first participation: Australia 2003'," explained Georgia Rugby Union vice president Zaza Kassachvili.

"So we say Georgian rugby was born with a Georgian father and French mother with godmother Australia and godfather England because our first World Cup game was against England.

"We know it is a baby now, but the baby can be growing. It just needs the parents to be thinking about the baby and now we need in the next couple of years to be very attentive to this baby.

Kassachvili, who admitted the World Cup had been " like a big dream " vowed to be present in every future tournament: " We cannot go back, Georgia must be present. The place of Georgia is in the top ten nations. "The Lelos - as they are fondly called – lived up to this promise and have appeared in every tournament since although they have always failed to get out of the group stages. They have though enjoyed great success in the European Nations Cup winning the tournament in 2001, 2008, 2009, 2011, 2012 and 2013 seasons. The bulk of the national squad are based in France, in both the Top 14 and lower divisions. In March 2015, they were ranked 14th in the world by the IRB. The draw for the 2015 tournament in England gives them a slim opportunity to progress beyond the group stage. Whilst including the current champions New Zealand, the next toughest teams are Argentina, ranked eight in the world, and Tonga, ranked just one place above them.

H – Humiliation

SHOCKS OR GIANT-KILLING ACTS are few and far between in the history of the World Cup but when they come they aren't forgotten. The first genuine shock came on 6 October, 1991 a date burned on the hearts of every Welsh rugby fan, the day a proud rugby nation lost to Western Samoa on their very own Cardiff Arms Park ground.

BELOW 6 Oct 1991- the day that Wales were humiliated at Cardiff Arms Park when they lost to Western Samoa

Proving a point after not being invited to the 1987 World Cup, Western Samoa won 16-13, at Cardiff Arms Park.

"We feel it was quite unfair for us not to be invited last time because we were the South Pacific champions in 1987," said Samoan rugby supremo Tate Simi.

"We've proved a point to some degree this time by qualifying ahead of Tonga, but what we want to do now is show that we deserve to be in the World Cup and not to have to go through the qualification rounds next time."

Samoa captain Peter Fatialofa called the three-point victory, "the greatest day in Samoan rugby history".

Wales captain Ieuan Evans was distressed. "We were devastated afterwards, and there were some pretty distraught fans there as well," he said.

"It showed how far we had deteriorated and let things slip, even if it took us another 10 years to do something about it.

"We probably got what we deserved after years of going through umpteen coaches and having a revolving-door policy with players. Not many people expected Wales to win the World Cup, but they didn't expect us to get knocked out at the pool stages.

"It was awful, horrible, something I wouldn't wish on my worst enemy."

The next big upset came in 1999 when odds-on favourites New Zealand, were knocked out at the semi-final stage by a rampant French team 43-31.

France were 24-10 behind before staging a comeback that stunned the rugby world, scoring 33 to seven from New Zealand, at Twickenham.

I – Ireland

IRELAND WERE ON THE WRONG end of their very own shock in 1999, when Argentina beat them in a quarter-final play-off that had the embarrassing repercussion of forcing them to qualify for the 2003 World Cup. "The Pumas exerted their normal squeeze up front and Ireland never looked comfortable," said Eddie Butler in The Observer. "Lansdowne Road would have been the place to be for a showdown with the French, but was not so attractive when it came to Argentina against France. It was a cultural and commercial opportunity lost. The Irish blew it."

They haven't always blown it but it is safe to say that Ireland have never over achieved at the World Cup. Quarter-finalists in 1987, 1991, 1995, 2003 and 2011, they have never gone on from there. France eliminated them in 1995 and 2003 and Australia in the opening two World Cup tournaments in 1987 and 1991. Ireland – who were early opponents of the concept of a World Cup - came closest to clearing the quarter-final hurdle when they came within a missed David Humphreys' drop goal

of winning their pool in 2003. When Humphreys' drop sailed wide - in the deciding match against Australia – they lost all chance of meeting Scotland in the last eight. Unfortunately for the Irish the 17-16 defeat to Australia pitted them into a quarter-final against a powerful France side.

"We are a devastated team at the moment," said the Ireland coach Eddie O'Sullivan after losing to Australia.

"We played all the rugby in the second half and deserved to win that game.

"But I am very proud of what they achieved, playing the world champions in their own back yard and taking the game to them every step of the way. If there was any justice we would have pulled that one off."

They failed to get out of a very tough " group of death " in 2007 but look to have one of the easiest pools in the 2015 tournament with France their only serious rivals. As current Six Nations' champions, another shock exit isn't on the cards.

ABOVE Brian O'Driscoll of Ireland chases a kick upfield during Ireland's quarter-final play-off against Argentina in 1999

RIGHT Neil Jenkins kicks for goal during the match against Argentina played at his beloved Millennium Stadium in 1999

J – Neil Jenkins

ONE OF THE GREATEST POINTS-SCORER in the history of rugby, Neil Jenkins may now be a World Cup legend but he wasn't always the darling of the Welsh fans, having to fill a No 10 jersey occupied by players like Barry John, Phil Bennett and Cliff Morgan.

Michael Lynagh was the world's leading points-scorer with 911 for the Wallabies before the man from Church Village rewrote the record books in a world cup pool game at the Millenium Stadium against Samoa in 2003. Perhaps nervous early on he hit a post with a penalty, before a conversion – to put Wales 7-3 ahead – took him past Lynagh's mark.

"I was always more concerned about the team," recalled Jenkins. "If the team scored four or five tries and I didn't kick any kicks and we won, I was happier than if I got the points and we lost. "

International coach Graham Henry commented: "I've coached for more than 30 years and you see a lot of very committed professionals. Neil Jenkins was right up there with the best of them.

"He was a role model for young rugby

players and deserved all the credit he got.

"He put hours and hours and hours of practice in and that made him the best goal-kicker in the world at that time."

Jenkins, who made his Wales debut at 19, ended his career with 87 caps and 1,049 points, the first player to go through the 1,000-point mark. He has since been overtaken as the highest rugby union test points scorer ever by the likes of Jonny Wilkinson (1246) and Dan Carter (1457 at the time of writing in April 2015).

K – John Kendall-Carpenter

THE SOMERSET HEADMASTER was one of the key driving forces behind the establishment of the Rugby World Cup when many nations were sceptical about starting a competition that they believed would lead to the abandonment of the game's amateur ethos. He was the English representative on the International Rugby Board when they agreed to host the first World Cup, in 1987. He was appointed the chairman of the steering committee to oversee the World Cup and was crucial in the structuring of rugby's new tournament.

Kendall-Carpenter spent a lifetime devoted to rugby and, before becoming instrumental in the birth of the World Cup, played for England 23 times and was president of the Rugby Football Union as well as chairman of the International Board. A proud Cornishman, at the time of his death he was involved in the 1991 World Cup.

LEFT John Kendall-Carpenter in 1989. During his playing years, he won 23 England caps

L – John and Martin Leslie

THE LESLIE BROTHERS WERE TWO of the most famous Kilted Kiwis and part of a long line of players who were born in one country, but represented another in the World Cup. The Leslies were born in New Zealand, qualifying for the Scotland team through their Scottish father.

The arrival of the Kilted Kiwis didn't receive universal approval, with former captain David Sole, believing it was a backward move to bring in players to the Scotland team who weren't born there.

"It was interesting in the way they arrived. I was surprised and at a loss as to how they came to fly across to Scotland and make their homes here," said Sole.

"And I was doubly surprised when John Leslie got the captaincy. I don't think there is any question about his capability as a player but it was very strange to appoint him captain.

"I think the Leslies would say, hand on heart, that they would love to play for New Zealand.

"We've gone too far to the opposite end of the scale where we are looking for rugby mercenaries."

But John Leslie, who scored a Six Nations try in just over nine seconds,

BELOW Martin Leslie in action during the first-round match between Scotland and Uruguay, 1999

against Wales retorted: "Leave the boys alone. We don't make up the rules. The critics are not looking at the whole picture. If they don't like it, they should change the rules.

"It became a personal thing - I felt persecuted by it. I don't need it. I'm just trying to do my best for whoever picks me."

Some other notable World Cup players who represented a country in which they weren't born include:

Mike Catt (England): South Africa
George Gregan (Australia): Zambia
Simon Shaw (England): Kenya
Victor Ubogu (England): Nigeria
Serge Betsen (France): Cameroon
Serge Blanco (France): Venezuela
Pieter De Villiers (France): South Africa
Marc Livremont (France): Senegal
Frankie Sheahan (Ireland): Canada
Dafydd James (Wales): Zambia

ABOVE John Leslie of Scotland charges forward against New Zealand at Murrayfield

M – Nelson Mandela

THERE ARE FEW MORE ENDEARING images in the history of sport - let alone rugby – than the one of South African President Nelson Mandela at the 1995 World Cup final. On 24 June, dressed in a green Springboks jersey – resplendent with a number six on the back – he appeared to present the Webb Ellis Cup to South Africa captain Francois Pienaar with an air of dignity and majesty that perhaps only he could have delivered. It is the photograph with which most rugby fans associate the Rugby World Cup and especially that magical tournament in 1995. The Rainbow Nation was in its infancy at that point but the handshake did so much for the country as a whole, coming as it did after an incredibly tense final, won in extra time by a Joel Stransky drop goal.

In Pienaar's book, Rainbow Warrior, he recounts perfectly the moment when the rugby world stood still.

"Then when President Mandela came out to present the Cup there was a hell of a lump in my throat," said Piennar. I wasn't aware that he was going to wear my shirt. When he handed me the Cup he said, 'Thank you very much for what you've done for South Africa.' And I said 'No, you've got it wrong. Actually, it's what you've done.'

"Sport in general has got the ability to be a unifier, not only in South Africa, but all over the world. Sport has got that mystique, it's such a powerful tool."

The whole event was made into a film, Invictus, by Clint Eastwood in 2009, with Matt Damon playing Pienaar and Morgan Freeman playing Mandela. Mandela's love affair with rugby didn't end in 1995 and he attended many more Test matches with the Springboks wearing his old prison number, 46664, on their shirts. His death in December 2013 saddened the world but his legacy as one of the greatest inspirational leaders that the world has ever known lives on." South Africa has been so blessed to have a man who put us on a very important road, and just hope the leaders following him will not only use his name for effect but because they truly believe in what he stood for, and build on that," said Pienaar.

N – New Zealand

THE NEW ZEALAND ALL BLACKS can lay claim to be being the best team in the history of the World Cup. Although they have won it the same number of times as Australia, they have appeared in more semi-finals.

Winners at the first tournament – in 1987 – it is incredible to think that such a great rugby nation had to wait some 24 years to get their hands on the Webb Ellis Cup again – defeating France in the final both times.

To be fair, they have stood over the World Cup like a colossus since it kicked off even though they have only won it twice.

In 1991, they lost their semi-final to Australia before winning the play-off for third. In 1995, as hot favourites they reached the final, before losing to hosts South Africa in extra time to a Joel Stransky drop goal.

They finished in fourth place in 1999, after losing their semi-final and then the third-place play-off game. In 2003, New Zealand were knocked out by hosts Australia in their semi-final, before finishing third.

The 2007 World Cup was their worst tournament, being knocked out in the quarter-finals by the host nation France; until this they were the only team to have reached the semi-finals of every tournament

The All Blacks have never lost a World Cup pool match, and have finished top of their pool in all seven tournaments.

They go into the 2015 tournament as the bookies' favourites but this is the World Cup and not the Tri-Nations tournament. Will it be a hat-trick of victories, putting them above all other world fifteens, and will they become the first team to ever retain the trophy?

ABOVE David Kirk holds up the Webb Ellis Cup after New Zealand beat France in the 1987 World Cup

O – Diego Ormaechea

THE 40-YEAR-OLD VETERINARY surgeon from Uruguay arrived at the 1999 World Cup as the oldest player ever to take part in the finals. Ormaechea was an inspiration to his side, leading them to a fabulous victory over Spain, 27-15, at Galashiels. When Ormaechea made his World Cup debut he'd been representing his country for 20 years and in fact scored their first try – from the back row – against Spain, in the battle of the 1999 minnows. Ormaechea made his debut in 1979 and in 1999 was amazed to be playing at a Rugby World Cup.

"This is not something I ever believed could happen," he said. "To be here is a dream come true at the end of my career and I am enjoying everything.

"It was good to be here, but to win our first match was even better. To score was an unbelievable moment for me. It opened the way for victory and rewarded the efforts made by the whole team.

"We don't get anything (money) for being here. We're from another world."

Ormaechea played his last Test in the 1999 pool, 39-3, defeat to South Africa and almost inevitably went on to become Uruguay's coach, taking them to the next World Cup, in 2003.

"It's a success for us just to be here," said Ormaechea, the coach, in 2003.

P – Pool System

EVER SINCE THE EMERGENCE OF the Rugby World Cup in 1987 they have persisted with a pool-based system to determine qualification for the knock-out rounds. But with the first World Cup being contested by 16 teams and the 2007 featuring 20, the organisers have tinkered with the way those pools have operated. The worst system was concocted for the 1999 tournament as the Rugby World Cup organisers decided – inexplicably – to divide the 20 teams into five groups of four. This meant the group leaders went through, as of right, the best runner-up joined them and then the six next best sides were sent into a new round: the Quarter-final play-offs. The system was a disaster because the play-off winners were then forced to play a quarter-final four days later and unsurprisingly all the play-off winners went out at the next stage, all hammered. Luckily sanity returned in 2003 when we returned to four groups of five, with the top two sides going through to the last eight. Bonus points were also introduced in 2003 with sides getting four points for a win and bonus points awarded for sides scoring four tries or more and for sides who lose by seven points or less. The bonus point system made no difference to the sides that actually qualified for the quarter-finals but it is a system adopted throughout the rugby world, to encourage attacking play. France and New Zealand were the only sides – in 2003 – to pick up a maximum of four bonus points, while qualifying.

BELOW Joost van der Westhuizen of South Africa passes to Percy Montgomery (15) in the 1999 Rugby World Cup quarter-final match against England

Q – Gonzalo Quesada

NOT MANY ARGENTINEANS HOLD World Cup records but prolific goal-kicker Gonzalo Quesada is certainly an exception, scoring an impressive 102 points at the 1999 World Cup, one more than the nearest player, Matt Burke. Quesada's impressive kicking display was one of the main reasons for Argentina's breakthrough in 1999, as they made the quarter-finals for the first time. And Quesada's achievement is all the more remarkable considering the fact that Burke's Australia stayed in for an additional two rounds. In 1999 Quesada – who won 36 caps for The Pumas – raised a few eyebrows as he rejected the use of a kicking tee, instead opting for sand to play the ball on.

"Each time I am using a tee, I feel I am limiting my possibility to give the ball the orientation that I want," said Quesada, who also scored 33 points at the 2003 World Cup, before retiring from Test rugby after that tournament. "With the sand I can mould my support how I want and choose my height with more or less sand. Each time I have used a tee I have missed my kick, but I will continue to train with them, if others can manage to do it. Why not me?"

He was nicknamed Speedy Gonzalo because of the time he took to take his kicks at goal, something that was restricted at the World Cup, as a 60-second limit for kicks at goal was introduced.

RIGHT Gonzalo Quesada kicks for goal during the World Cup Pool D match between Argentina and Samoa in 1999

R - Huw Richards

THE WELSHMAN HAD THE unenviable distinction of becoming the first player to be sent off in a World Cup match when he was dismissed in the 1987 semi-final against New Zealand. Wales were demolished in the game, as New Zealand were unstoppable, winning 49-6. It was one of the few occasions on which a sending-off had little or no bearing on a Test match. Richards was shown the red card by Kerry Fitzgerald, the Australian referee, in the final minutes of the game for punching Gary Whetton. The punch caused a brawl and the unfortunate Richards was then knocked semi-conscious by All Blacks No 8 Wayne Shelford who should have been – but was not – dismissed as well. A further 14 sending offs have occurred in the following world cups (although there were none in 2003) with Wales having the distinction of having the first and last person to be sent off in the history of the tournament when captain Sam Warbuton was dismissed for a controversial tackle in the 2011 – conincidentally both Dragons sawred in the semi-finals!

The full list of World Cup sinners is:

1987 Huw Richards:
For Wales against New Zealand
David Codey:
For Australia against Wales
1991 Pedro Sporleder:
For Argentina against W.Samoa
Mata'afa Keenan:
For W.Samoa against Argentina
1995 James Dalton:
For South Africa against Canada
Gareth Rees:
For Canada against South Africa
Rod Snow:
For Canada against South Africa
Feleti Mahoni:
For Tonga against France
1999 Marika Vunibaka:
For Fiji against Canada
Dan Baugh:
For Canada against Namibia
N Ta'ufo'ou:
For Tonga against England
Brendan Venter:
For South Africa against Uruguay
2003 None
2007 Hale T Pole:
For Tonga against Samoa
Jacques Nieuwenhuis:
For Namibia against France
2011 Paul Williams:
For Samoa against South Africa
Sam Warbuton:
For Wales against France

S - South Africa

THE SOUTH AFRICANS HAD THE distinction of being one of the nations that voted for the establishment of a World Cup – in 1985 – in the knowledge they would not be allowed to take part.

Their enthusiasm could probably be attributed to the success they had enjoyed since arriving on the Test scene in the 1920s, only losing on a regular basis to the New Zealand All Blacks.

The sporting boycott caused by South Africa's apartheid political regime meant that the Springboks missed the 1987 and 1991 World Cups but they were back with a bang in 1995.

South Africa were finally readmitted to international rugby in 1992 with an historic Test against New Zealand in Johannesburg on 15 August and it was-n't long before the International Rugby Board was awarding the third World Cup to the Rainbow Nation.

The All Blacks came into the tournament as the undisputed world's number one side but they had managed to peak in between World Cups.

The South African form was far from conclusive in the opening rounds and they only scraped into the final after beating France in a rain-sodden semi-final in Durban.

But once they made the final it was as if the gods of rugby had conspired in their favour. Even though the All Blacks had hammered England in their semi-final and had the seemingly unstoppable Jonah Lomu in their ranks, the Springboks triumphed.

It took them until extra time to do so, Joel Stransky kicking the unforgettable drop goal to hand them a 15-12 victory. A nation – and perhaps a continent – celebrated! They have gone on to play a major part in subsequent tournaments, winning in 2007 (see chapter two – part six), finishing third in 1999 and making the quarter finals in 2003 and 2011. They should easily escape from their pool in the 2015 World Cup and will be expected to make the semi's at least.

BELOW South African fans enjoy the opening ceremony of the 1995 World Cup prior to their team's opening match against Australia

T- Television

BROADCASTERS HAVE ENJOYED A huge influence over the game of rugby union and at the World Cup, often dictating the kick off times of matches. But the coverage in the media has been crucial to the development of the tournament, which started when the sport of rugby union was a strictly amateur affair.

The first tournament – in 1987 – was light years away from the event in 2003. In 1987 600,000 people passed through the turnstiles with 300 million in 17 countries watching the action on television.

By 2003 two million spectators attended the matches (average of 38,282 per game) during the Rugby World Cup, watched by a cumulative world television audience of 3.5 billion, broadcast in 205 countries. This included 400 jumbos of international tourists and 500,000 Australian bed nights giving plenty of rest to the 40,000 overseas visitors.

The internet grew during the course of the tournament. Few companies had websites in 1987 but by 2003 rugbyworldcup.com had 495 million hits over the Tournament including 44.5 million

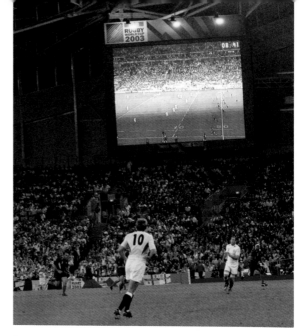

hits on the day of the Final.

ITV will be the UK and worldwide host broadcaster for the 2015 event, having signed a deal to broadcast the 2011 and 2015 RWC tournaments. It will show every match from the tournament live in the UK on ITV and ITV4.

Welsh language broadcaster S4C will show all of Wales' pool games (and the opening match), along with one game from each corresponding knockout fixture. In Ireland, TV3 and sister channel 3e will broadcast the matches.

ABOVE Television captures England's 2003 semi-final against France

U – The Underwoods

TWO OF THE MOST FAMOUS brothers to play in the World Cup, Tony and Rory Underwood enjoyed varying degrees of success for England in the 1990s when both were Test players. Rory was always the senior partner of the double act – not just in age – and had a prolific record for England at World Cups running in 11 tries.

Rory's full England career brought a remarkable 49 tries in 85 Tests, and he was made an MBE in 1992 for his services to rugby.

The Underwood brothers were the first to play in the same England team together since 1937 when they started against South Africa in 1992, in a 33-16 win for England, Tony scoring a try.

Rory certainly had the more memorable of World Cup careers, making his debut in 1987, excelling at the tournament four years later, and ending his career in 1995.

Rory was robbed of the chance to win the World Cup for England in 1991, David Campese knocking on, perhaps

CENTRE Rory and Tony Underwood were the first brothers to represent England at the same time since 1937

deliberately, a pass from Peter Winterbottom to Underwood, that if caught would have given the wing a clear run to the line.

Tony in contrast is hardly likely to forget his only World Cup campaign – in 1995 – but probably for the wrong reasons.

Tony was selected for the semi-final, in Cape Town, and asked to mark the played well all season and scored a try in the win over Australia, so I was hardly going to say: 'I can't handle Jonah.'

"The only saving grace I can take from the whole thing is that I wasn't steamrolled by Jonah for his four tries. Sadly that happened to all my team-mates after I got caught out of position."

In that semi-final Tony's brother Rory restored some family pride with two tries in the game to ensure some respectability to the scoreline.

The 2003 World Cup featured nine sets of brothers, including twins, some playing for different countries. Dimitri and Gregoire Yachvili represented France and World Cup debutants Georgia respectively, while Brent and Matt Cockbain were in the squads of Wales and Australia.

Another set of siblings who played for different countries at RWC 2003 were Rodney and Steven So'oialo, who represent New Zealand and Samoa respectively.

Argentina had two sets of brothers in their ranks – in 2003 - in twins Felipe and Manuel Contepomi and Juan de la Cruz Fernández Miranda and Nicolás Fernández Miranda.

colossus that is Jonah Lomu.

It is fair to say that Lomu won that battle, scoring four tries and throwing Underwood – like a rag doll – off the field at one point.

"I remember Jack Rowell (coach) and Will Carling (captain) asking me if I could handle Jonah on my own," Underwood recalls.

"I was feeling fairly confident. I'd

V – Dr Roger Vanderfield

THE CHAIRMAN OF THE International Rugby Board in the 1980s, Dr Roger Vanderfield, was another man who was crucial to the establishment of the Rugby World Cup as one of the most important sports tournaments in the world. When the proposal for a World Cup arrived at the door of the IRB Dr Vanderfield's support was vital, as there were a number of dissenting voices in the rugby world.

Vanderfield was an international referee, officiating in 15 Test matches between 1956 and 1974, ending his career in the middle with New Zealand's 16-6 victory over Australia in Sydney. Following his death in September 2008, he was posthumously inducted into the IRB Hall of Fame for his pivotal role in the creation of the Rugby World Cup.

W – William Webb Ellis

THE RUGBY SCHOOL STUDENT IS credited with being the father of the game of rugby union, although there is little or no evidence to suggest that he actually "picked up the ball and ran with it" as legend tells us. The game certainly has its origins at Rugby School and many of its former pupils left an indelible mark on the history of the game, moving from country to country to help establish rugby. It is far more likely – according to Jed Smith, the eminent historian at the Museum of Rugby - that a group of Rugby schoolboys established the game, deriving rugby from one of the ball-based games already played at the school. Pupils would meet at the end of each day to discuss rules and how the game was developing. Webb Ellis's grave – in the south of France – has become something of a shrine and the heritage he brings to the game made his name the obvious choice for the World Cup trophy, which is called the Webb Ellis Cup. The cup – which is made of gilt silver - was made

by Garrard and Co of London and modelled on a 1906 trophy made by Carrington and Co of London, designed by Paul de Lamerie.

The Australians gave it the nickname 'Bill' when they won it in 1991 and in 1999 they ran a 'Bring Back Bill' campaign.

The claim that Webb Ellis invented the game didn't appear until after his death, explaining how hard it was to corroborate, and in 1895 a Rugby School investigation turned up no evidence to support the theory that boys were allowed to play the game with their hands.

Rugby union was finally established as a credible sport in 1871 when a common set of laws was established at a meeting to form the Rugby Football Union, where there would clearly have been some former Rugby School pupils. The first international – against Scotland – followed soon after. In 1871 representatives from rugby clubs across the country met to form the Rugby Football Union and draw up their own common code of laws.

ABOVE The grave stone of William Webb Ellis with the Webb Ellis Cup on it at Menton Cemetery

X – Cross Coders

THROUGHOUT THE HISTORY OF rugby union the game has lost a significant number of players to the professional sport of rugby league. This changed in 1995 when union shed its amateur ethos, leading to a number of league players signing for union clubs. In the 2003 World Cup final former league players scored both tries, Lote Tuqiri getting the first for Australia and England's Jason Robinson diving over in the corner to put his side back in the lead. With the dominance of league in Australia it isn't surprising that two other former league players – Mat Rogers and Wendell Sailor – also played for the Wallabies in that World Cup campaign. There were a number of other former league players dotted around the other teams at the tournament, most notably Wales outside-half Lestyn Harris. England also used former Great Britain coach Phil Larder as their defence coach in their successful 2003 campaign, and when he left the job in 2006 his place was taken by his former league colleague, Mike Ford.

Y – Youngest and other records

THE YOUNGEST EVER PLAYER TO appear in a World Cup match was Thretton Palamo, of the USA, who was just eight days past his 19th birthday when he faced South Africa in 2007.

Taylor Paris (born October 6 1992) of Canada was younger when he was named in his country's 2011 squad with their pool matches all taking place before his 19th birthday but sadly he never got on the pitch!

The youngest player ever to appear in a final was Jonah Lomu, who, although looking much older, was just 20 years and 43 days old when he played for New Zealand against South Africa in June 1995.

The youngest player to actually win the World Cup Final was Francois Steyn, from South Africa, who was aged 20 years and 159 days when he helped beat England in 2007.

The oldest player to appear in a Final was Brad Thorn, of New Zealand, who was aged 36 years and 262 days when he

played against France in October 2011; while four years previously Diego Ormaechea had become the oldest player to have taken part in the tournament when at 40 years and 26 days he played for Uruguay in a pool match against South Africa.

Our own Jason Leonard has made the most appearances with 22 matches at the tournament; while Jonny Wilkinson has the most overall points, 277, in the final stages after taking part in four world cup tournaments.

Z – Zimbabwe

AT THE 1987 WORLD CUP THE 16 competing nations were invited, rather than having to qualify. With South Africa subject to a sporting boycott due to the presence of the apartheid political regime in their country, an African substitute was sought and finally agreed as Zimbabwe, a position they held in 1991, although the side failed to win any matches in those first two World Cups. Once South Africa were readmitted in 1995, they were given the first African place and although a second African country is now admitted – as part of the qualification process – Zimbabwe have never made it.

In 2015, Namibia will have qualified as the second African country for the fifth successive World Cup, although they have yet to win or draw a game in 15 attempts.

Looking on the bright side, they won five matches in qualifying for this year's tournament but once again it will be South Africa that carries the hopes for the continent on their shoulders.

RIGHT Andy Ferreira of Zimbabwe passes out of the scrum in the game against Ireland, during the 1991 World Cup

World Cup Stars

15 players who have lit up rugby's greatest show on earth

SERGE BLANCO
Country: *France*
Position: *Full-back / Wing*
Test Caps: *93*
Test Points: *233*
World Cups (2): *1987 and 1991*

IF ONE PLAYER SUMMED UP THE flair, spirit and general joie de vivre of the French rugby team in the 1970s and 80s, it was full-back Serge Blanco.

A 60-a-day smoker through his 12-year Test career, Blanco was grace personified – with a cheeky side – while a veritable brick wall as the last line of defence.

Perhaps the greatest player France ever produced, he scored one of the greatest tries the World Cup has even seen, when France beat Australia to reach the first World Cup final, in 1987.

The artisan of the French team in two World Cup campaigns, the first – in 1987 – where they made that final, Blanco left the World Cup with one of its most endearing memories.

"In that classic semi-final France launched a long, sweeping movement as only they can, involving forwards and all their backs," recalled The Observer's Eddie Butler.

"Serge Blanco had to finish it. The full-back had been complaining of hamstring trouble, but still mustered the speed to make it to the line at the corner, despite the tackle of the burly Wallaby hooker Tommy Lawton."

Unfortunately for Blanco and Les Bleus they couldn't finish the job by beating New Zealand in the final and by the time the 1991 tournament came around Blanco was captain.

Once again France fell short, this time suffering a far more unpalatable defeat, losing in the quarter-final to England, in Paris. Blanco retired once the tournament was over.

But even in his last game, even though France lost, he stayed in the headlines. Two minutes into the game Blanco landed a flurry of punches on England wing Nigel Heslop, who was late into a tackle.

"The referee warned me that I would go for another punch, but he said that he was a good friend of mine and it was his duty to see that I did not leave the field in that way," Blanco said.

Blanco, who was born in Venezuela, racked up a then world-record 38 tries in a career that started when he joined Biarritz in 1975.

"My game, such as it was, was 'instinctif, spirituel'," Blanco explained.

"I could not coach at any senior level: I have had my share of stress and ten-

sion caused by rugby, and I have seen it become even more pressurised and maniacal for coaches than even for the players themselves, the ones who are actually going out to perform."

One of the greatest full-backs the world has ever seen Blanco was quick enough to make his Test debut on the wing and play 11 more times there for France.

In a ground-breaking career he won 93 caps for France. After retiring Blanco stayed involved with his beloved Biarritz Olympique, eventually becoming the club president, presiding over their French Championship wins in 2002 and 2006. Blanco was also president of the French League until December 2008. In March 2009 he suffered a heart attack but recovered after surgery.

ABOVE Serge Blanco dashes through the Welsh defence in 1991

OPPOSITE Blanco was a master with ball in hand and with the boot

DAVID CAMPESE

Country: *Australia*
Position: *Wing*
Test Caps: *101*
Test Points: *315*
World Cups (3): *1987, 1991 and 1995*

THE ULTIMATE SHOWMAN, DAVID
Campese played in two Rugby World
Cups, leaving an indelible mark on the
1991 tournament, where he was instrumental in Australia lifting the Webb
Ellis Cup for the first time. His knock-
on (whether deliberate or not) in the
final certainly helped Australia to victory but it was in the semi-final where
he showed his genius. Australia had
won a heart-stopping victory against

BELOW David
Campese makes a
break during the 1991
Australia v New
Zealand semi-final
match

Ireland in the quarters and their reward was a clash with holders New Zealand. But when the going got tough, Campo took centre stage. Described by his captain in 1991, Nick Farr-Jones, as "pure genius" Campese took that semi-final by the scruff of its neck to knock the All Blacks out. Voted Player of the Tournament in 1991, the New Zealand game was unquestionably his finest in the green and gold. Campese had already scored tries against Argentina, Wales and Ireland and it only took him 12 minutes to cross the line against the All Blacks crossing from wing to first receiver and drifting over the line on the perfect angle and with the game just 35 minutes old he created a magnificent score for Tim Horan. Tearing through the New Zealand defence he threw an outrageous over the shoulder pass to Horan, and Australia were in the final. "There's always Campo, and when you've got a player like that in your team you always know probably something is going to happen," said All Blacks coach Alex Wylie. "He did it again – he just pulled that one out. An individual like that: one day he could probably blow it, but the other four days he could make it. It was just unfor-

tunate he made it against us."

Campese wasn't blessed with devastating speed but he possessed the guile to unlock any defence in the rugby world.

A motor-mouth of the highest order, Campese may not have scored in the 1991 final win over England but many credit him with convincing England to ditch their forward-dominated game plan for a more expansive outlook, which many consider was crucial to their downfall.

He didn't take long to announce himself on the world stage. Given his debut at 19 against New Zealand in Christchurch he was handed the task of marking Stu Wilson, one of the world's best at the time.

"He left Wilson standing. He totally stood him up," explained Australia coach Bob Dwyer.

"At once we knew it was a very rare person we had on our hands. It wasn't the fact that he beat him, or even the way that he did, that was so stunning. It was that he had the daring to try it in the first place."

When Campese retired his 64 Test tries were a world record, overtaken in 2006 by Japan's Daisuke Ohata.

JOHN EALES

Country: *Australia*
Position: *Second row*
Test Caps: *86*
Test Points: *173*
World Cups (3): *1991, 1995 and 1999*

THROUGHOUT JOHN EALES'S 10-year reign in the Australia second row the man from Brisbane was called 'Nobody'.

Strange you may think for one of the most successful rugby players in the history of the game; a player who won every international honour available.

But you can understand where the moniker came from when you appreciate he was called 'Nobody' because, well…'Nobody is perfect'.

Perfection was a state that Eales achieved many times in his career. Certainly, no one could accuse him of being the archetypal second row.

Not only was he one of the world's best in the lineout and loose but he also scored a remarkable 173 points in Test matches, as he became an accomplished goalkicker. That total ensured he was the highest scoring forward in Test history.

Unfortunately for his opponents he was as happy winning the ball at the front of a lineout, in a scrum, ruck or in the backline making try-saving tackles. His athleticism set him apart from the majority of second-row forwards.

Eales also timed his retirement to perfection. In 2001, the season he helped Australia to a series win over the Lions, two years after their second World Cup victory, and while still at the top of his game, he made his announcement.

Eales agonised over the decision for some time but said: "At the end of the Lions series I sat back and reassessed my playing future and I decided that I would throw everything into this Tri-Nations campaign before stepping down for good."

His departure was felt throughout all Australian society and not just in the rugby world, prompting prime minister John Howard to say: "I wish to record my admiration for the magnificent contribution that John Eales has made to the game of rugby, and to Australian and international sport.

"John Eales has been an inspirational leader, an outstanding and courageous player, and an example to all in the way he has conducted himself on and off the field."

Off the field, Eales was awarded the Order of Australia Medal in 1999 for his services to rugby and the community.

His Test career started in 1991 – in Brisbane – against Wales and he ended after winning everything that was possible in the game: World Cup (twice), Tri-Nations, Bledisloe Cup and that series victory over the Lions.

At state level he played 112 times for Queensland, kicking off at the Brothers Rugby Club.

Australia won 41 of his record 55 Tests as captain following his appointment to the job, for the first time, in 1996.

Perhaps we should have guessed all those years ago that his was destined to be one of the most successful careers in the history of the game as the Wallabies won that first Test match by a record margin, 63-6. From then on the records just kept falling.

But of all those records that fell he must surely be proudest of his two World Cup victories.

Eales played in all of Australia's matches as they lifted the Webb Ellis Cup with a 12-6 defeat of England, in 1991. Playing more like a flanker he marauded around the field, the baby of the Wallabies' pack.

And eight years later Eales was there once again, but this time as the side's captain as they trounced France 35-12 in the final.

GRANT FOX

Country: *New Zealand*
Position: *Outside-half*
Test Caps: *46*
Test Points: *645*
World Cups (2): *1987 and 1991*

BEHIND EVERY GREAT TEAM THERE is usually a great goalkicker. Think of England in 2003 and you see Jonny Wilkinson, Australia in 1991 and it is Michael Lynagh, and of course Joel Stransky is inextricably linked to the 1995 Springboks' World Cup win.

But standing above all those legendary goalkickers – in World Cup terms - is Grant James Fox, one of the key reasons why New Zealand ruled the rugby world in the late 1980s and early 1990s.

When New Zealand won the 1987 World Cup they scored 298 points in six matches, 126 of them by fly-half Fox. He scored 26 against Fiji and 17 in their 29-9 victory in the final against France.

That 126-point total set a tournament record that still stands today.

Born in New Plymouth, Fox became a New Zealand legend after attending world famous Auckland Grammar School, and going on to set new standards, across the world.

In a mould-breaking 11-year career for Auckland and the All Blacks he kicked a remarkable 1,621 goals, at an incredible average of almost 14 points a game for both teams.

He was never an outside-half with the air of a Barry John or Phil Bennett but his radar boot could not be denied and he was in fact a far better runner than most people ever gave him credit for. His tactical kicking allied with his rugby brain delivered as many games for the All Blacks as his almost unerring goalkicking.

But he took some time to convince the All Blacks selectors of his merits. First picked for the 1985 tour of South Africa – which was later abandoned due to apartheid – he finally made his debut in Argentina in 1985.

He had to wait until the first game of the 1987 World Cup for his home debut and he barely looked back until his final game – in 1993 – after he'd masterminded an historic win over the British and Irish Lions.

"He is an incredible bloke, such a perfectionist and so analytical. He explained the mechanics of goal-kicking and changed my approach to the whole business," explained Andrew Mehrtens, one of the All Blacks who tried to fill Fox's No 10 shirt.

Fox was only three years and 12 matches into his Test career – in 1988 - when he broke the old New Zealand points scoring record, held by SuperBoot Don Clarke. He only needed six matches to reach his century of points for New Zealand.

LEFT Grant Fox the goal-kicking phenomenon who excelled in the 1987 tournament

GAVIN HASTINGS

Country: *Scotland*
Position: *Full-back*
Test Caps: *61*
Test Points: *667*
World Cups (3): *1987, 1991 and 1995*

HOLLYWOOD ACTOR MEL GIBSON starred in the famous film about Scottish legend, William Wallace, called Braveheart.

BELOW Gavin Hastings in 1993

And although Wallace is still revered across the length and breadth of Scotland in rugby circles they had their very own Braveheart in the shape of Gavin Hastings.

Readers of Scotland's Daily Record newspaper voted him the second greatest Scot of all time – behind Wallace – to emphasis the position he had attained north of the border.

And even though Hastings' last game was a World Cup quarter-final defeat to New Zealand he was still carried – shoulder high – off the pitch by Scotland supporters.

He'd scored 15 points as the Scots lost 48-30, and afterwards New Zealand captain Sean Fitzpatrick led the tributes.

"Gavin Hastings is certainly the best full-back in the world at the moment," said Fitzpatrick. "We began our international careers in the same year and so I'm a contemporary of his. Gavin has been a fine player and a fine ambassador, not just for Scottish rugby, but also for the game of rugby as a whole.

"He's shown his class again in this World Cup and he can definitely hold his head high."

Politicians even joined in the clamour to verbally pat the big man on the back. Sir Hector Monro, the Scottish office minister with responsibility for sport added: "I would like to extend my personal thanks for the wonderful memories with which he has left us all and for the manner in which he has conducted himself in victory and defeat throughout his very distinguished career."

Hastings – who started his club rugby for Watsonians - finished his career with a record 667 points for Scotland and a record 61 caps, the cap mark later overtaken by brother, Scott.

And minutes after that last match he was as modest as ever, preferring to talk about the team and the supporters, rather than himself.

"The feeling is one of immense pride, captaining Scotland at the World Cup and leading them for the last three seasons. It has been magnificent. At times it has been very hard, but you can put away the bad times and savour the good times," Hastings said.

"I'd like to pay tribute to the Tartan Army. The support that we have received has been fantastic and they certainly make themselves heard, that's for sure.

"Coming out here to the World Cup was an ambition of mine and it has been a great experience that will live with me for a long, long time. But now is the time to move on to new things.

"So far as today is concerned, I want to say how proud I am of the way that the boys came back in those last 10 minutes, when I'm sure it must have looked to most people as if New Zealand would score 60."

His record of 227 points in World Cup finals (three tournaments between 1987 and 1995) still stands today.

And in Six Nations terms he went out on a big high. In 1995 he scored a try as Scotland beat France – in Paris – for the first time since 1969.

Hastings – who was instrumental in Scotland's 1990 Grand Slam – wasn't just taken to the hearts of Scottish rugby fans as he captained the 1993 Lions close to an historic triumph in New Zealand.

Lions historian Clem Thomas remembered a gregarious captain on the 1993 trip "There is no man more respected for his abilities both on and off the field than this delightful Scot, who is the epitome of the rugby man; brave, resolute, adventurous and one who loves a party," said Thomas.

After ending his Test career, just as rugby union turned professional, he dabbled with American football when he quit rugby, turning out for the Scottish Claymores.

ABOVE Gavin Hastings clashes with Philippe Saint Andre of France, 1995

MARTIN JOHNSON

Country: *England*
Position: *Second-Row*
Test Caps: *84*
Test Points: *10*
World Cups (3): *1995, 1999 and 2003*

BELOW Martin Johnson of England lifts the Webb Ellis Cup aloft after England won their match against Australia, 2003

IT IS SAID THAT YOU NEVER KNOW exactly what you have until it is gone. And this phrase was never more aptly used to describe the influence of Martin Johnson on both the England and Leicester teams.

Both sides, and the man himself, would have talked down Johnno's influence – once he was gone – but the bare facts remain that with Johnson at the helm England won the World Cup in 2003 and Leicester won back-to-back Heineken Cup titles in 2000 and 2001.

Without him England spent the three years following their World Cup triumph spiralling down the world rankings and Leicester struggled to even make the knock-out stages of Europe's top competition.

Of course other players retired when Johnson left the international scene and a certain Jonny Wilkinson was blighted by injury. But Johnson was the heartbeat of both the England and Leicester teams of the early 21st century.

On that incredible day in Sydney – when England won the World Cup - everyone remembers that Wilkinson kicked the winning drop goal but few remember it was Johnson who drove the ball up the middle for the final time so Wilkinson could be set and Matt Dawson could deliver the perfect pass; another example of a man engaging in a selfless act on behalf of the team.

Regarded by many as the greatest English rugby player of all time, the World Cup final was the last in a long line of great games played by the Leicester lock.

He made his England debut as an 11th hour replacement for Wade Dooley – in 1993 - and then promptly put in a great display as England beat France 16-15.

And apart from the Grand Slams in both 1995 and 2003, when Johnson was colossus, there were the two games – against New Zealand and Australia – in the months before the World Cup win that defined him and England as the world's number one.

Against New Zealand, England's pack was reduced to six players by the sin-binning of Neil Back and Lawrence Dallaglio, but Johnson held them together.

"You saw Martin Johnson at his absolute best in that 10-minute period. His leadership was just inspirational," said England coach Clive Woodward.

And of course Johnson's view of his heroics was typically self-effacing. "I just told them to get down and shove," Johnson revealed.

Long before Johnson lifted the Webb Ellis Cup above his head – in Sydney – he was guaranteed his place in rugby folklore.

Already an England legend, in 2001 he became the first man to captain the British and Irish Lions on successive tours.

He skippered a winning side in 1997 and four years later came within a whisker of the same result, before the side lost the third Test, 29-23, and the series 2-1.

"The 1997 tour was special for everybody involved, and as captain, Martin was at the head of that. He was an inspirational leader," explained former team-mate Lawrence Dallaglio.

"This was his first big captaincy job, and he did it fantastically well. He didn't alienate anybody. You had strong characters on that tour - Keith Wood, guys like Rob Wainwright and David Young - who had captained their countries, and everybody felt part of it. If there was a meeting, Martin would want some senior players there. He liked to hear other people's ideas and was comfortable involving others in the leadership of the team.

"What I will remember is the warrior, the guy who, more than anything, wanted to win. I liked his style too, totally unfussy and very tough."

He may have been raised in the Midlands with a mother who took him long-distance running to build up his stamina, but some of his tough edges were knocked off in a short trip to New Zealand.

As a teenager Johnson decided to try his hand at New Zealand rugby, in Colin Meads' King Country, and he even made the New Zealand Under-21 side before returning to England for his incredible career.

The New Zealanders would have loved for him to have settled in their country and played for the All Blacks. Luckily for England he chose to return home.

Allied to his success with England and the Lions he had an unprecedented run with his only professional club, the Leicester Tigers.

Under his leadership Leicester won four consecutive English League titles and two Heineken Cups.

He was the popular choice to manage England when he was appointed in July 2008 and in 2011 won the Six Nations tournament. He resigned in November of that year after England's poor performance in the world cup.

ABOVE Martin Johnson drives ahead during the Rugby World Cup semi-final match between England and France

MICHAEL JONES

Country: *New Zealand*
Position: *Flanker*
Test Caps: *55*
Test Points: *56*
World Cups (2): *1987 and 1991*

ONE OF THE KEY REASONS WHY New Zealand romped through the 1987 World Cup, destroying everyone in their path was flanker, Michael Jones.

Although a devoted Samoan when he

BELOW Michael Jones runs with the ball during the Bledisloe Cup game against Australia, 1991

made his Test debut in 1987 Samoa weren't even part of the World Cup family, so – with him living in New Zealand - it was a natural progression for him to play for the All Blacks.

Latterly he has become a key figure in the welfare of Polynesians working and living in New Zealand, particularly with his work at Auckland University.

He was taken to the heart of the New Zealand public as they voted him the third greatest All Black, of all time, behind Colin Meads and Sean Fitzpatrick.

Rugby World Magazine named him the best openside in the history of the sport, picking him in their Team of the Millennium.

And Wellington's Evening Post newspaper described him as "rugby's greatest role model".

He did much to define the role of the openside flanker we see in rugby today. He had great ball skills, allied with a powerful physique and the uncanny ability to follow the ball around the field.

Former New Zealand coach John Hart who coached Jones at both Auckland and with the All Blacks called him "almost the perfect rugby player."

Nicknamed 'The Iceman' due to his

cool attitude under fire, Jones saw his career interrupted by two serious knee injuries, which prevented him from adding to his 55 caps.

Following his exploits on the field Jones was persuaded to move into coaching, where he became the spiritual leader of the Samoan team, first as John Boe's number two and more recently as head coach.

"In the Pacific we eat, sleep and drink rugby. It is so entwined with their sense of who they are, and their sense of pride, and being Samoan, Tongan, or Fiji, or even, you know, Cook Island, Niuean, Tokelauan, because it's just such a big part of the culture now," Jones explains.

Jones's impact on the game was all the more remarkable considering the religious stand he made stating that he would never play rugby on a Sunday.

This ensured that he missed a number of key games, but such was his ability the All Blacks continued to select him when he was available.

But as a man of principle he refused to break a promise he once made. "I had to make my mind up on the subject when I was 16 or 17 and I'm so grateful to the coaches and players I was involved with who accepted it," said Jones in the New

Zealand Herald. "But I know there were times when I apologised to players [who had covered for me] and some coaches probably thought it was a bit strange at first.

"You don't put God in a box in deciding what you do and don't do on Sundays. I know that I would probably struggle to get a contract now. For a young player in the situation now it would be a case of talking to the right people and praying about it - go to the final word. In the end it is a very personal thing."

That pledge even restricts his duties as a coach and if Samoa are scheduled to play on a Sunday Jones takes a "step back" from active coaching on match day.

"When I stopped playing rugby, people soon forgot the player and one thing I'd like to be remembered for is the one person who put God before rugby," he says.

"I feel that people who would never have heard about God, have done so because of my stand, because it's brought attention to it. I've been able to show people that there obviously is a God who must exist or else someone wouldn't be prepared to do that."

Doing the extraordinary was Jones's mantra, whether on or off the pitch.

ABOVE Michael Jones in action during a 1991 World Cup match against the USA

NICK FARR-JONES

Country: *Australia*
Position: *Scrum-half*
Test Caps: *63*
Test Points: *37*
World Cups (2): *1987 and 1991*

AUSTRALIA COACH BOB DWYER IS a man rarely short of an opinion, rarely short of an analytical view on a player. So when he describes a player's influence as "immeasurable" it is wise to sit up and take notice.

Dwyer was forced into such a claim when asked to consider the career of scrum-half Nick Farr-Jones, the man who lifted the Webb Ellis Cup in 1991.

Dwyer handed Farr-Jones the Australia captaincy in 1988 – after the sacking of Andrew Slack - and once he had decided to hang up his boots in between the 1991 and 1995 World Cups, Dwyer said: "His contribution is immeasurable, almost impossible to put into words. All you can say is that he could not have done more."

What Farr-Jones did do was help mastermind a remarkable transformation in the fortunes of the Australian rugby team.

No-hopers in the 1970s, Farr-Jones was one-third of the Holy Trinity – with Michael Lynagh and David Campese – that spearheaded their reversal of fortunes to such an extent they lifted the World Cup twice, in 1991 and 1999.

The three stars first announced their presence in the rugby world in 1984 as Australia completed a Glam Slam tour of Britain and Ireland, then going on to dominate on the world stage. Farr-Jones made his Test debut on that tour, kicking off his international career with Mark Ella outside him.

A natural leader, Farr-Jones was the obvious choice to skipper the side after they had finished fourth at the first World Cup. From the moment he had the armband the campaign to go much further in 1991 started in earnest.

That campaign didn't go that smoothly until a 1990 victory in New Zealand made the team believe they could become the world's number one side.

He followed some legends into the Wallabies' number nine shirt (John Hipwell and Ken Catchpole) showing leadership qualities that set him apart in the history of Australian rugby.

A sniping runner and fearless defender, Farr-Jones developed a great pass off either hand.

Central to his abilities was the half-back

partnership he formed with Lynagh. Together in 47 Tests the two men set a world record for a half-back partnership.

Farr-Jones tried to retire in 1992 only to be called back for one last crack at the Springboks a year later. The series was won, clinched with a 19-12 victory and Farr-Jones could depart in style.

"Before we ran on, it (Farr-Jones' retirement) was in the back of our minds," Australian captain and man-of-the-series Phil Kearns said.

"One of the brothers has gone. That is disappointing but we are glad we gave him a win. We did not want to let him down."

After he retired, Farr-Jones – who captained Australia a then record 36 times - stayed in public life, with a successful business career, and in 1999 became an elected councillor in Sydney.

He can be seen as rugby commentator on Sky Sports and is the chairman of NSW rugby.

ABOVE Nick Farr-Jones was devastating from the base of the scrum as he shows here in the 1991 semi-final against New Zealand

JASON LEONARD

Country: *England*
Position: *Prop*
Test Caps: *114*
Test Points: *5*
World Cups (4): *1991, 1995, 1999 and 2003*

WHEN JASON LEONARD RAN OUT on to the pitch at Sydney's Telstra Stadium on 16 November 2003 few people in the crowd realised the exact significance of his appearance.

He was after all only sent on as a blood replacement for England tighthead Phil Vickery.

Nothing unusual about that and when Vickery was bandaged up he returned to the action, sending Leonard back to the bench.

But in replacing Vickery, even just for ten minutes, Leonard had chalked up his 112th cap for England, overtaking Philippe Sella's previous world record of 111 for one country.

Although Leonard only made a handful of those appearances off the bench it was, in many ways, fitting for the former carpenter from Barking. The appearance was understated and that suited the modest Leonard.

The rugby world soon woke up to the gravity of his appearance and although England went on to beat France and make it to their second World Cup final, England coach Clive Woodward made a special mention of the player afterwards.

"I hope what Jason has achieved won't be forgotten in the aftermath of this game," said Woodward.

Leonard's achievement is clearly all the greater because he played all his rugby in the front row, either on the loose or tighthead, where careers grow shorter and shorter.

Woodward added: "Jason has been an outstanding ambassador for the game on and off the pitch.

"All of his caps for England have been earned on merit and his contribution towards four Grand Slams and our World Cup win has been massive over the last 14 years.

"He will be sorely missed by his team-mates in the England squad, the coaches, management and of course the fans."

The supporters, as Woodward intimated, took 'Our Jase' to their hearts. A down to earth grafter, so many England fans could relate to Leonard and the efforts he had made to make it to the top.

The "Fun Bus" (as he is known) endeared himself to his many of legions of fans by devoting some pages in his autobiography to his "All-time drinking XV" from team-mates past and present. Only Leonard would have done that!

Leonard – who made his Test debut in Argentina in 1990 - wasn't even that lucky with injuries and one neck problem, developed in May 1992, saw him have to overcome damaged vertebrae. He underwent surgery to remove a piece of

his hip bone and graft it to the top of his neck.

But four Grand Slams, four World Cup campaigns and three British and Irish Lions tours later he could walk away from the game with his head held high.

Leonard started his career at Barking, moving to Saracens and in 1990 his rugby journey took him to Harlequins, where he stayed until he retired in 2004.

Leonard was lucky enough to end his Harlequins career on a high, coming on as a late substitute as the Londoners won The Parker Pen Cup and soon after he made his final bow at Twickenham, for the Barbarians against England.

He captained England twice, the first time in 1996 against Argentina, a match he rounded off with his one and only Test try.

After taking a break from rugby, Leonard – who was awarded an OBE for his services to rugby - resisted the temptation to move into coaching and finally, in 2006, became a member of the RFU Council, the body that runs English rugby.

BELOW Jason Leonard displays a commemorative number 112 jersey after setting a new world record of 112 international apppearances during the Rugby World Cup semi-final between England and France

BRIAN LIMA

Country: *Samoa*
Position: *Wing / Centre*
Test Caps: *64*
Test Points: *140*
World Cups (5): *1991, 1995, 1999, 2003 and 2007*

TO PLAY IN ONE WORLD CUP IS AN honour. To play in two or three puts you in an elite club, but in 2007 Brian Lima became the first man to play in five World Cups. Simply the stuff of legends! In the 2003 World Cup he broke the record of any player for consecutive appearances in the finals, running out for his 15th successive World Cup match when Samoa faced England in the pool stages. He bettered the record with a final game against South Africa. But at the next World Cup he went one better and achieved a world record mark.

Originally a wing, Lima made his debut for Manu Samoa back in 1990 and moved into the centre as his career progressed after making his tournament debut in Western Samoa's 16-13 historic win over Wales in their first World Cup match in 1991.

The youngest player at the 1991 World Cup, Lima developed a fearsome reputation for his tackling, earning himself the nickname of 'The Chiropractor'.

One of those legendary hits came in the last World Cup when South Africa fly-half Derick Hougaard felt the full force of a Lima tackle as he attempted to juggle a pass from Joost van der Westhuizen.

But before Hougaard could react Lima came hurtling at him with a tackle that went down as one of the moments of the 2003 World Cup.

"I was winded a bit, and it all went dark for a while," Hougaard explained.

"I had to lie on the ground for a few minutes just to get my breath back.

"I am still here so that is a good sign but it was definitely the hardest tackle I have ever taken."

Lima played provincial rugby for Auckland and for both Auckland Blues & Otago Highlanders in the Super 12, before moving to Bristol in the

Guinness Premiership.

And at Bristol he found a big fan in head coach Richard Hill. "He was devastating when he has had the ball and he made an impact with the ball in hand.

"Brian brought international experience to our backline and was a massive physical presence."

Now retired, he was inducted into the IRB Hall of Fame in 2011.

JONAH LOMU

Country: *New Zealand*
Position: *Wing*
Test Caps: *63*
Test Points: *185*
World Cups (2): *1995 and 1999*

THE GIANT ALL BLACKS WING LEFT an indelible mark on the Rugby World Cup playing in just two tournaments – 1995 and 1999 – but still establishing himself as the competition's leading try-scorer, with 15. When he arrived – with a bang – at his first World Cup little was known of this 6ft 4in, 18st 8lb player of Tongan heritage, but four tries in the semi-final – against England – put an end to his anonymity. Lomu was rugby's first global superstar, a player guaranteed to pull in the crowds wherever he went.

Against England he went around and over some of the best players in the rugby world and ensured his place in the history of the game.

His undoubted ability prompted England captain Will Carling to call Lomu "a freak" and it was the biggest compliment Carling could pay the big man after the most devastating performance in the history of the Rugby World Cup.

It wasn't as if Carling should have been surprised by Lomu's impact. On his World Cup debut – against Ireland – he scored two tries as New Zealand won 43-19.

Lomu and New Zealand couldn't repeat the trick in the final, losing 15-12 to South Africa, but no-one was left in any doubt over the identity of the man of the tournament.

Keith Quinn, one of New Zealand's most famous commentators summed up his global appeal.

"Jonah was the most sensational player at any time, from any country, from any part of rugby history," said Quinn.

"If you travel to any faraway country where other sports are their national game and say you are from New Zealand, the locals will say two things: they will say 'All Blacks' and after that 'Jonah Lomu'. They don't say anything else. Lomu is a household name."

He first announced himself on the world stage at the 1994 Hong Kong Sevens tournament and his love of Sevens led to him winning a gold medal at the 1998 Commonwealth Games.

Lomu – who started his rugby career as a flanker before moving into the backs - continued to haunt England and effectively knocked them out of the 1999 tournament as well, scoring a crucial try that ensured they couldn't win their pool.

The records just kept coming for Lomu, starting it all off on his first appearance in the famous black jersey against France in 1994. At 19 years and 45 days he became the youngest All Black of all time.

And his achievements are all the more amazing if you consider he powered through his career with a debilitating kidney disease.

"Towards the end of 2003 it was hard to get through training - and the darkest point was when a doctor told me there was a possibility I could end up in a wheelchair," Lomu explains, even though he made an impressive 63 appearances for New Zealand.

That illness, which affected Lomu throughout his whole career, led to him having a kidney transplant in 2004, miss-ing the 2003 World Cup as he had been put on dialysis three times a week.

Incredibly Lomu came back from the transplant to play professional rugby in Wales for the Cardiff Blues in the 2005-06 season.

His dream of playing in the 2007 World Cup ended when he failed to get a Super 14 contract for the 2006-07 season, although his bravery in actually making it back on to the pitch, made him one of the most admired sporting figures of his generation.

BELOW Jonah Lomu in action during a World Cup match against Tonga in 1999

MICHAEL LYNAGH

Country: *Australia*
Position: *Outside-half*
Test Caps: *72*
Test Points: *911*
World Cups (2): *1991 and 1995*

A WORLD CUP WINNER IN 1991, Michael Lynagh did more than most to ensure the Wallabies made the final of the second Rugby World Cup. Gordon Hamilton looked to have put Ireland through in the quarter-final with a late try but with just seconds left Lynagh completed an incredible move to score and hand his side a 19-18 victory.

"It captivated people back home. I heard endless stories of people kicking their cats or booting the dog after Gordon Hamilton scored to put Ireland ahead with four minutes left," recalled Australia captain Nick Farr-Jones "I heard of some who even went to bed assuming the game was lost."

Farr-Jones was off the pitch and even suggested afterwards that had he been on the field the outcome could have been very different.

Australia were handed a penalty and instead of kicking it, Lynagh took a tap penalty and set off down the field, David Campese going just short, before Lynagh dived over.

"I'd come off injured and, sitting in the stands, thinking we were done," Farr-Jones added.

"Michael Lynagh treated the situation very differently to how I would. I would have read the riot act but he asked the ref how long was left and then said he would kick long.

"That (decision to run it) took guts and the rest is history as he went on to score.

"For sure we were lucky. One minute we were down and out of the World Cup and the next we were somehow back in it and on our way to face New Zealand."

Lynagh made his Test debut in 1984, retiring after Australia were knocked out of the 1995 World Cup, at the quarter-final stage, by England. Capped 72 times. Lynagh ended his career as the world's leading points-scorer with 911, a record later bettered by Neil Jenkins. At the advent of professionalism Lynagh joined Saracens and helped them win the Tetley's Bitter Cup. He is now an analyst for Sky Sports.

OPPOSITE Michael Lynagh of the Wallabies in action during the Rugby World Cup semi-final match between Australia and Ireland, 1991

FRANCOIS PIENAAR
Country: *South Africa*
Position: *Flanker*
Test Caps: *29*
Test Points: *15*
World Cups (2): *1991 and 1995*

WHEN SOUTH AFRICA WON THE 1995 World Cup the team managed to unite a country behind them. The symbol of that team and the man inextricably linked with the Springboks victory was captain Francois Pienaar.

BELOW Francois Pienaar tries to gather the ball during the semi-final against France in 1995

Born in Vereeniging in 1967, Pienaar became not only one of the most important sporting figures in the new South Africa but he also transcended sport in June 1995, when South Africa staged and won the World Cup.

Just three years after Nelson Mandela made his legendary Walk to Freedom and apartheid fell, the picture of President Mandela presenting the Webb Ellis Cup to Pienaar is one of sport's most endearing images.

And when Pienaar reflected on the victory, he knew the Springboks had won the cup not just for the 60,000 fans in Ellis Park but for the whole South African nation of 43 million people.

"I've said it many times that no Hollywood scriptwriter could have written a better script," Pienaar recalls at BBC online.

"It was just unbelievable on the streets of South Africa. For the first time all the people had come together and all races and religions were hugging each other. It was just wonderful.

"Nelson Mandela said 'thank you very much for what you've done for South Africa' but I said 'thank you for what you've done'. I almost felt like hugging him but it wasn't appropriate, I guess.

"Then I lifted the trophy which was unbelievable. I can't describe the feeling as I wouldn't do it justice. If I had the chance I would have stood there forever."

President Mandela summed up Pienaar's influence inside and outside rugby when he wrote the forward to his autobiography, Rainbow Warrior. "Amongst sports leaders, Francois Pienaar stands out. It was under his inspiring leadership that rugby, a sport previously associated with one sector of our population and with a particular brand of politics, became the pride of the entire country," said President Mandela. Due to the sporting boycott that surrounded apartheid South Africa missed the first two World Cups and even though they hosted the event in 1995, they came into the tournament seeded ninth.

Pienaar had come to national attention as part of the Transvaal side that won the Currie Cup in 1994; the same year Rugby World magazine voted him their International Player of the Year.

Pienaar was relieved of the Springboks captaincy a year after the World Cup victory, by new coach Andre Markgraaff.

But South Africa's loss – as Gary Teichmann replaced Pienaar – became

England's gain as he arrived at north London club Saracens.

Pienaar brought success to Saracens as they lifted the English (Tetley's Bitter) Cup, finishing twice in the league's top three.

"Initially we were going to stay only a year. Finally we stayed six. It was a fantastic time," said Pienaar.

After he retired, Saracens owner Nigel Wray made Pienaar the Saracens chief executive, a post he held until 2002 when he returned to live in South Africa.

He was a pundit for ITV during the Rugby World Cups of 2007 and 2011.

ABOVE Springboks captain Francois Pienaar receives the Webb Ellis Cup from South Africa president Nelson Mandela, after the 1995 final

GARETH REES

Country: *Canada*
Position: *Outside-half*
Test Caps: *55*
Test Points: *487*
World Cups (4): *1987, 1991, 1995 and 1999*

WHEN CANADA CAPTAIN GARETH Rees strode out onto the Beziers' Stade Mediterranee on 2 October 1999, when the Canucks played France, he became the first person to play in four Rugby World Cups, making his tournament debut – as a teenager – in 1987.

Widely regarded as the greatest Canadian player he represented his country 55 times and even though his final cap came in 1999 his total of 487 Test points is still a Canadian record.

He retired after the 1999 World Cup but not before registering a 100% record with the boot in that tournament, slotting all 19 kicks attempted. His last Test match was the 72-11 defeat of Namibia.

In his World Cup career Rees chalked up 120 points and is one of the legends of the tournament.

"I've played in four of them, it's been a huge part of my life," Rees said. "I suppose I was quite lucky, I was pretty young at the first one and went straight through to 1999.

"It was an awesome experience and pretty spectacular to see how the Rugby World Cup has developed and how the game was changing around the event, so a lot of positives and a few negatives."

"With the advent of the Rugby World Cup people don't realise how important

RIGHT Gareth Rees clears under pressure

it is to a region like North America where you don't have the day to day coverage of rugby, a World Cup is something the press and sponsors can get behind."

The highlight of Rees's World Cup trips was Canada's campaign in 1991, when they made the quarter-finals and showed they had the potential to move into the elite.

They lost to New Zealand and Rees said: "The 1991 quarter-final for us was just special to be there and take Canada to that place in the rugby world which is something you only dreamt of as kids growing up in Canada.

"To actually be in a quarter-final stage, albeit maybe a bit of a mismatch, against a very powerful All Blacks side was special. We got stuck in and didn't concede. To be on that stage in a Canadian jersey was pretty special."

He was one of Canada's rugby warriors, a player brought up in the amateur era and even when the game turned professional he still kept the spirit of rugby in his soul.

"My dad always taught me that sport isn't about the score or who scored what goal, basket or try when," said Rees in the Times Colonist.

"He taught me that sport is about peo-

ple. Yes, you want to be a success in the league statistics and you want your team on top of the standings and all that. But he told me never to lose sight of the importance of sport in other ways. That's why I never have trouble in selling sport to kids because I know what you can get out of it. It can keep you out of trouble and broaden your horizons through travel, even if it's just to the Okanagan for a tournament. You can't put a price tag on that."

Rees's esprit de coeur took him to a number of clubs, playing for Oak Bay Castaways, Merignac, Newport, Wasps, Oxford University, Harlequins, Bedford, and he was also proud of his performances for the world famous Barbarians.

In October 2011, Rees received arguably his greatest honour with induction to the IRB Hall of Fame one of the few ex-players from outside the top rugby-playing nations.

BELOW Gareth Rees (left) passes the ball, flanked by Canadian winger Winston Stanley (right) during the first-round match between Fiji and Canada, 1999

JONNY WILKINSON

Country: *England*
Position: *Outside-half*
Test Caps: *91*
Test Points: *1,179*
World Cups (3): *1999, 2003 and 2007*

BELOW Jonny Wilkinson celebrates after the final match between Australia and England, 2003

THE ENGLISH NATION HELD THEIR breath at 11.22am (GMT) on Saturday, 22 November 2003, as Matt Dawson fired a pass back to Jonny Wilkinson in Sydney's Olympic Stadium, in the World Cup final between England and Australia. The scores were tied at 17-17 but the nation needn't have worried as Wilkinson swung his weaker right boot to land the drop goal, win the World Cup and instantly become the most famous rugby player on the planet.

Following the World Cup win Wilkinson endured an injury run that may have finished most players, failing to pull an England shirt in the following three years,

although he did play international rugby for the British and Irish Lions in 2005.

Wilkinson had played a cameo role in the world cup of 1999, when England lost in the quarter-finals, but again took centre stage for the England side that reached the Final in 2007.

Due to a non-contact ankle injury sustained in training, Wilkinson was not included in the teams for the opening games against the USA and then South Africa. He returned to score 24 points in a win over Samoa and helped England to victory against Tonga which put them through to the quarter-finals. During England's 12–10 quarter final win against Australia, in which he scored all of England's points, Wilkinson became the world cup's leading point scorer with 231 points, surpassing Gavin Hastings of Scotland.

He continued to play a major role in England's defence of the World Cup by kicking nine points, including a last gasp 40-metre drop goal, in their 14–9 semi-final victory over France. In the Final, on 20 October at the Stade de France, South Africa won the Webb Elliss Cup in a game where Wilkinson slotted home two penalties but missed two drop kick attempts. He was one of only four play-

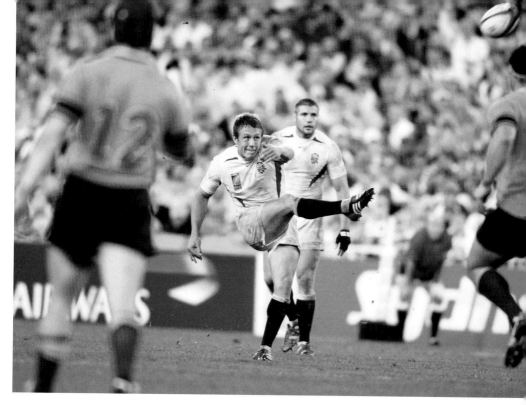

ers to have started both the 2003 and 2007 Rugby World Cup Finals, the other three being Phil Vickery, Jason Robinson and Ben Kay.

He played his club rugby union for Toulon following a dozen seasons in the English Premiership with the Newcastle Falcons. He bowed out as a superstar at Toulon having won two Heineken Cups in his final two seasons and the Top 14 Final in which he kicked 15 out of the 18 points which beat Castres in his final match of his career.

Wilkinson was signed up as the star pundit for ITV during their coverage of the world cup in 2015.

ABOVE Jonny Wilkinson kicks the winning drop goal to give England victory in extra time during the World Cup final between Australia and England, 2003

Chapter 5

2015
Rugby World Cup Preview

THE WIDER WORLD THOUGHT AN emerging rugby nation like Japan should have hosted the eighth tournament, but Rugby World Cup Limited also assessed bids from South Africa, England and Italy. The organization reviewed the bids and recommended to the IRB in 2009 that England should run the event, although the Japanese will finally get to host the world's third-biggest sporting spectacle in 2019. As there were concerns that the 2011 event would generate a loss, there's no doubt that England's bid, which predicted raising £300 million for the IRB through broadcasting, sponsorship, merchandising and tournament fees, was given a boost by being the strongest financially.

The infrastructure in England is well-suited to a World Cup and stadia such as Twickenham (82,000 capacity),

Wembley (90,000), the Olympic Stadium (54,000) and the Millennium Stadium in Cardiff (74,500) will all host games. Other venues include the Etihad Stadium in Manchester (56,000), St James' Park in Newcastle (52,500), Elland Road in Leeds (38,000) and Villa Park in Birmingham (43,000). Five more stadia with capacities ranging between 12,500 (Sandy Park in Exeter) and 32,000 (Leicester City) will host the remaining games.

Qualification for the tournament was based on how well the side did at the 2011 World Cup, with the top three teams from each of the four groups receiving automatic invitations. The remaining eight teams had to qualify through regional tournaments. In all, 80 countries entered the qualifying tournament and they completed 184 matches.

ABOVE New Zealand will be prepared to go to war to keep hold of the trophy they waited so long to hold... Can anyone dethrone them?

The teams that have made it to the World Cup are: Australia, England, Wales, Fiji and Uruguay (Pool A); South Africa, Samoa, Scotland, Japan and the United States (Pool B); New Zealand, Argentina, Tonga, Georgia and Namibia (Pool C); and France, Ireland, Italy, Canada and Romania (Pool D).

Although the Six Nations will be used by the northern hemisphere sides to experiment with the best player combinations, a series of warm-up games are scheduled throughout August and September. The tournament itself then kicks off with England against Fiji at Twickenham in West London on Friday September 18. The quarter-finals will be played on October 17 and 18 and will be shared between the Millennium Stadium in Cardiff and Twickenham.

Twickenham will host both semi-finals the following weekend and then the final on October 31. As hosts, England will be expected to perform well, and coach Stuart Lancaster's side have been building nicely towards the tournament after a poor showing in New Zealand in 2011.

South Africa were the only side to beat the All Blacks in the 2014 Rugby Championship but their 27-25 win at Ellis Park did little to persuade neutrals that the defending champions won't still be the team to beat in England. The Rainbow Nation should qualify for the knockout phase of the tournament with Scotland or Samoa, while Argentina should join the All Blacks from their group.

Australia managed a draw with the Kiwis in their opening match of the Rugby Championship but they conceded 51 points in the return fixture and were also beaten by England in the autumn internationals. They're looking to rebuild throughout 2015 and should qualify from their group, although with Wales, England and Fiji alongside them, this pool is bound to throw up a surprise result.

Pool D could also provide a few scares for the bigger teams: France should top the group but Ireland, Italy and Canada will all feel they have a chance to progress in the tournament via the harder route for finishing second. Only Romania will struggle to qualify.

POOL A	POOL B	POOL C	POOL D
Australia	South Africa	New Zealand	France
England	Samoa	Argentina	Ireland
Wales	Scotland	Tonga	Italy
Fiji	Japan	Georgia	Canada
Uruguay	United States	Namibia	Romania

RUGBY WORLD CUP 2015 MATCH SCHEDULE

M	DATE	TEAM 1	TEAM 2	POOL	VENUE
1	18/09/2015	England	Fiji	A	Twickenham
2	19/09/2015	Tonga	Georgia	C	Gloucester
3	19/09/2015	Ireland	Canada	D	Cardiff
4	19/09/2015	South Africa	Japan	B	Brighton
5	19/09/2015	France	Italy	D	Twickenham
6	20/09/2015	Samoa	USA	B	Brighton
7	20/09/2015	Wales	Uruguay	A	Cardiff
8	20/09/2015	New Zealand	Argentina	C	Wembley
9	23/09/2015	Scotland	Japan	B	Gloucester
10	23/09/2015	Australia	Fiji	A	Cardiff
11	23/09/2015	France	Romania	D	London (O/S)
12	24/09/2015	New Zealand	Namibia	C	London (O/S)
13	25/09/2015	Argentina	Georgia	C	Gloucester
14	26/09/2015	Italy	Canada	D	Leeds
15	26/09/2015	South Africa	Samoa	B	Birmingham
16	26/09/2015	England	Wales	A	Twickenham
17	27/09/2015	Australia	Uruguay	A	Birmingham
18	27/09/2015	Scotland	USA	B	Leeds
19	27/09/2015	Ireland	Romania	D	Wembley
20	29/09/2015	Tonga	Namibia	C	Exeter
21	01/10/2015	Wales	Fiji	A	Cardiff
22	01/10/2015	France	Canada	B	Milton Keynes
23	02/10/2015	New Zealand	Georgia	C	Cardiff
24	03/10/2015	Samoa	Japan	B	Milton Keynes

London (O/S) = London's Olympic Stadium

M	DATE	TEAM 1	TEAM 2	POOL	VENUE
25	03/10/2015	South Africa	Scotland	B	Newcastle
26	03/10/2015	England	Australia	A	Twickenham
27	04/10/2015	Argentina	Tonga	C	Leicester
28	04/10/2015	Ireland	Italy	D	London (O/S)
29	06/10/2015	Canada	Romania	D	Leicester
30	06/10/2015	Fiji	Uruguay	A	Milton Keynes
31	07/10/2015	South Africa	USA	B	London (O/S)
32	07/10/2015	Namibia	Georgia	C	Exeter
33	09/10/2015	New Zealand	Tonga	C	Newcastle
34	10/10/2015	Samoa	Scotland	B	Newcastle
35	10/10/2015	Australia	Wales	A	Twickenham
36	10/10/2015	England	Uruguay	A	Manchester
37	11/10/2015	Argentina	Namibia	C	Leicester
38	11/10/2015	Italy	Romania	D	Exeter
39	11/10/2015	France	Ireland	D	Cardiff
40	11/10/2015	USA	Japan	B	Gloucester
41	**17/10/2015**	**W Pool B**	**RU Pool A**	**QF1**	**Twickenham**
42	**17/10/2015**	**W Pool C**	**RU Pool D**	**QF2**	**Cardiff**
43	**18/10/2015**	**W Pool D**	**RU Pool C**	**QF3**	**Cardiff**
44	**18/10/2015**	**W Pool A**	**RU Pool B**	**QF4**	**Twickenham**
45	**24/10/2015**	**W QF1**	**W QF2**	**SF1**	**Twickenham**
46	**25/10/2015**	**W QF3**	**W QF4**	**SF2**	**Twickenham**
47	**30/10/2015**	**L SF1**	**L SF2**	**3rd/4th**	**London** (O/S)
48	**31/10/2015**	**W SF1**	**W SF2**	**Final**	**Twickenham**

Chapter 6

2015
Rugby World Cup Venues

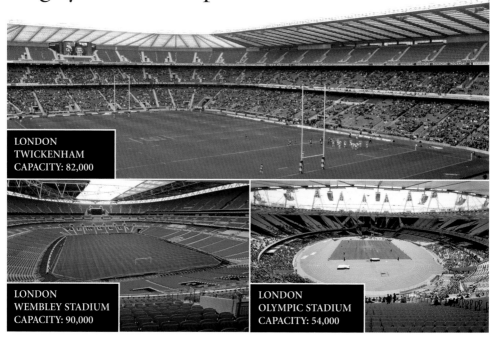

LONDON
TWICKENHAM
CAPACITY: 82,000

LONDON
WEMBLEY STADIUM
CAPACITY: 90,000

LONDON
OLYMPIC STADIUM
CAPACITY: 54,000

MANCHESTER
MANCHESTER CITY STADIUM
CAPACITY: 56,000

CARDIFF
MILLENNIUM STADIUM
CAPACITY: 74,500

BIRMINGHAM
VILLA PARK
CAPACITY: 42,788

LEICESTER
LEICESTER CITY STADIUM
CAPACITY: 32,262

BRIGHTON
BRIGHTON COMMUNITY STADIUM
CAPACITY: 30,750

MILTON KEYNES
STADIUM MK
CAPACITY: 30,500

EXETER
SANDY PARK
CAPACITY: 12,500

GLOUCESTER
KINGSHOLM STADIUM
CAPACITY: 16,500

LEEDS
ELLAND ROAD
CAPACITY: 37,900

NEWCASTLE
ST. JAMES' PARK
CAPACITY: 52,387

COMING SOON

A REVIEW OF THE RUGBY WORLD CUP 2015:

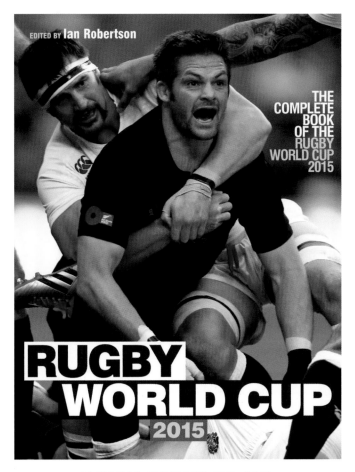

WWW.G2ENT.CO.UK

The pictures in this book were provided courtesy of the following:

GETTY IMAGES
101 Bayham Street, London NW1 0AG

WIKIMEDIA COMMONS

Design & Artwork by: Alex Young

Published by: G2 Entertainment Limited

Publishers: Edward Adams & Jules Gammond

Written by: Paul Morgan and Liam McCann

Foreword by Ian Robertson

With thanks to Adrian Stephenson